Coping With Chronic Illness

Coping With Chronic Illness

A Cognitive-Behavioral Therapy Approach for Adherence and Depression

Workbook

Steven A. Safren • Jeffrey S. Gonzalez • Nafisseh Soroudi

OXFORD
UNIVERSITY PRESS

2008

OXFORD
UNIVERSITY PRESS

Oxford University Press, Inc., publishes works that further
Oxford University's objective of excellence
in research, scholarship, and education.

Oxford   New York
Auckland   Cape Town   Dar es Salaam   Hong Kong   Karachi
Kuala Lumpur   Madrid   Melbourne   Mexico City   Nairobi
New Delhi   Shanghai   Taipei   Toronto

With offices in
Argentina   Austria   Brazil   Chile   Czech Republic   France   Greece
Guatemala   Hungary   Italy   Japan   Poland   Portugal   Singapore
South Korea   Switzerland   Thailand   Turkey   Ukraine   Vietnam

Copyright © 2008 by Oxford University Press, Inc.

Published by Oxford University Press, Inc.
198 Madison Avenue, New York, New York 10016

www.oup.com

Oxford is a registered trademark of Oxford University Press

ISBN 978-0-19-531515-8 (pbk.)

Printed in the United States of America
on acid-free paper

About Treatments*ThatWork*™

One of the most difficult problems confronting patients with various disorders and diseases is finding the best help available. Everyone is aware of friends or family who have sought treatment from a seemingly reputable practitioner, only to find out later from another doctor that the original diagnosis was wrong or that the treatments recommended were inappropriate or perhaps even harmful. Most patients or family members address this problem by reading everything they can about their symptoms, seeking out information on the Internet, or aggressively "asking around" to tap knowledge from friends and acquaintances. Governments and health care policy makers are also aware that people in need don't always get the best treatments—something they refer to as "variability in health care practices."

Now health care systems around the world are attempting to correct this variability by introducing "evidence-based practice." This simply means that it is in everyone's interest that patients get the most up-to-date and effective care for a particular problem. Health care policy makers have also recognized that it is very useful to give consumers of health care as much information as possible, so that they can make intelligent decisions in a collaborative effort to improve health and mental health. This series, "Treatments*ThatWork*™," is designed to accomplish just that. The latest and most effective interventions for particular problems are described in user-friendly language. To be included in this series, each treatment program must pass the highest standards of evidence available, as determined by a scientific advisory board. Thus, when individuals suffering from these problems or their family members seek out an expert clinician who is familiar with these interventions and decides that they are appropriate, they will have confidence that they are receiving the best care available. Of course, only your health care professional can decide on the right mix of treatments for you.

This workbook describes a cognitive-behavioral treatment that targets both depression and adherence in individuals living with chronic illness. It has been shown that individuals with chronic medical conditions are prone to depression, which can compromise their ability to follow the medical program recommended by their doctors. If you are infected with HIV or have diabetes, high blood pressure, heart disease, cancer, asthma, or any other type of long-term illness and you suffer from depression, the program outlined in this workbook can help. Based on the principles of cognitive-behavioral therapy, the program described will teach you the skills you need to overcome your depression, while simultaneously improving your adherence to your medical regimen. You will learn problem-solving methods and strategies for changing your negative thoughts, as well as relaxation procedures and breathing techniques to deal with symptoms and side effects. Most important, you will learn the necessity of getting to your medical appointments, communicating with your doctor, taking your medication on time, and properly storing your medicine and supplies. Throughout treatment you will work with your therapist to deal with barriers that may prohibit you from taking the best possible care of yourself. Keeping up with your self-care behaviors will not only make you feel better physically but will also improve your mental health.

This program is most effective when carried out in collaboration with your clinician.

David H. Barlow, Editor-in-Chief
Treatments *ThatWork*™
Boston, Massachusetts

Contents

List of Figures and Worksheets   *ix*

Chapter 1   Introduction   *1*

Chapter 2   Overview of the Program   *17*

Chapter 3   Life-Steps   *35*

Chapter 4   Activity Scheduling   *57*

Chapter 5   Adaptive Thinking (Cognitive Restructuring):
Part I   *67*

Chapter 6   Adaptive Thinking (Cognitive Restructuring):
Part II   *81*

Chapter 7   Problem Solving   *93*

Chapter 8   Relaxation Training and Diaphragmatic
Breathing   *101*

Chapter 9   Review, Maintenance, and Relapse Prevention   *111*

About the Authors   *119*

Figures and Worksheets

Cognitive-Behavioral Model of Depression   *21*

Center for Epidemiologic Studies Depression Scale (CES-D)   *26*

Weekly Adherence Assessment Form   *28*

Motivational Exercise: Pros and Cons of Changing   *31*

Progress Summary Chart   *32*

Homework Rating Chart   *33*

Center for Epidemiologic Studies Depression Scale (CES-D)   *36*

Weekly Adherence Assessment Form   *37*

Adherence Goals Worksheet   *42*

Example of Completed Medical Regimen Schedule   *47*

Medical Regimen Schedule   *48*

Improvement Graph   *52*

Life-Steps Action Items   *54*

Center for Epidemiologic Studies Depression Scale (CES-D)   *58*

Weekly Adherence Assessment Form   *59*

Positive Events Checklist   *62*

Activity Log   *64*

Example of Completed Activity Log   *65*

Center for Epidemiologic Studies Depression Scale (CES-D)   *68*

Weekly Adherence Assessment Form   *69*

Thought Record   *76*

Example of Completed Thought Record Up to Cognitive
Distortions Column   *77*

Center for Epidemiologic Studies Depression Scale (CES-D)   *82*

Weekly Adherence Assessment Form   *83*

Example of Completed Thought Record   *90*

Thought Record   *91*

Adaptive Thinking: Developing a Rational Response   *92*

Center for Epidemiologic Studies Depression Scale (CES-D)   *94*

Weekly Adherence Assessment Form   *95*

Problem-Solving Sheet   *99*

Center for Epidemiologic Studies Depression Scale (CES-D)   *102*

Weekly Adherence Assessment Form   *103*

Breathing Retraining and Progressive Muscle Relaxation Practice
        Log   *108*

Treatment Strategies and Usefulness Chart   *112*

One-Month Review Sheet   *115*

Example of Completed Troubleshooting Your Difficulties
        Worksheet   *116*

Troubleshooting Your Difficulties Worksheet   *117*

Chapter 1 *Introduction*

Background Information and Purpose of This Program

This workbook describes a cognitive-behavioral treatment that targets both depression and adherence in individuals living with chronic illness and depression. Our approach is based on cognitive-behavioral therapy (CBT), which is a type of psychotherapy that has been extensively researched and found to be an effective treatment for depression and other mental health problems. CBT is a relatively short-term therapy that focuses on how you are thinking, feeling, and behaving in the present. This approach emphasizes the role of thoughts (cognitions) in causing and/or maintaining problems such as depression and aims to improve negative patterns of thinking. CBT also focuses on changing patterns of behavior through increasing pleasurable activities and opportunities for positive events. We have designed this workbook to be used as part of treatment with a therapist who is familiar with cognitive-behavioral approaches. There is an accompanying therapist guide that goes along with this program that your therapist may use to guide treatment. In this section we present background information regarding the development of the program, information about types of depression, and information about the importance of maintaining proper adherence to a medical regimen. Typically, when using this workbook as part of a therapy program with a therapist, you will begin with the first treatment session outlined in chapter 2. This background section is meant to provide additional information for you to consider before seeking or while beginning your treatment.

Our treatment approach is based on a large body of research that has been conducted to evaluate the efficacy of CBT as a treatment for depression in the context of chronic illness. The reason we developed this specific treatment program is that depression is very common among individuals who have chronic medical conditions and can make it much more difficult to manage a medical illness. Research has shown that patients with both chronic medical conditions and depression can experience greater distress and sometimes worse medical outcomes than those with medical conditions who do not have depression. Although there is some emerging evidence that depression can impact illness through associated biochemical changes, one of the reasons for worse medical outcomes for individuals with depression is that having depression makes it harder to practice good self-care behaviors, including medical adherence. In fact, there is a good deal of research that demonstrates that patients with chronic illness and depression have a harder time taking their medications, keeping medical appointments, following diet and exercise recommendations, and so forth, than patients with chronic illness who do not have depression.

In order to better understand how depression could negatively impact one's ability to practice good self-care and medical adherence, it's important to understand what is involved in the self-management of chronic illness. It's also important to understand what exactly we mean when we use the term *depression,* as it involves much more than just feeling sad. In this section we go over these terms and then present the rationale for our belief that our treatment approach could be helpful for patients who are having problems with depression in the context of a chronic illness.

What Is "Adherence"?

Adherence refers to the degree to which a patient follows (or adheres to) a medical regimen. Different medical conditions might require adherence to a variety of behaviors, such as taking medicines, exercising, following a diet, and keeping regular medical appointments. Ideally, the appropriate medical regimen for a given patient is established collaboratively between a medical provider and the patient. We use the term *adherence* instead of *compliance* because we believe that it is important for a patient to understand the rationale behind the regimen and to be an active participant in the decision to follow it. *Compliance* implies that the doctor or medical provider is coming up with "instructions" on his or her own and that the patient simply needs to follow "doctor's orders." In chronic illness, adherence is a long-term undertaking, and it requires much more than passive compliance from the patient. The treatment of the illnesses that we discuss in the pages that follow requires active involvement on the part of the patient in order for treatment to be successful. We find that adherence is best maintained if the medical regimen is something that is agreed on between both the medical provider and the patient, such that the patient fully understands the benefits and consequences of following the treatment plan.

Even when treatment plans are established collaboratively, depression can make it much harder to perform necessary self-care behaviors. Additionally, depression often reduces motivation and interest, and this can make it difficult to put in the effort required to stick to a medical regimen over time.

What Is Depression?

There are several different types of depression. The most common forms are major depression, dysthymia, and the bipolar disorders, which have features of mania (periods of feeling so full of energy or so irritable that it causes problems). Major depression and dysthymia are considered forms of "unipolar" depression, as they do not involve the symptoms of mania, which are the hallmark of the bipolar disorders. Brief definitions are as follows:

- Major depressive disorder is characterized by single or recurrent episodes of excessive sadness and or loss of interest in things in which a person would normally be interested. Usually this happens for 2 weeks or longer and is accompanied by other symptoms, such as sleep problems, guilt or feelings of worthlessness, concentration problems, loss of energy, increased or decreased appetite, decreased interest in sex, and even hopeless feelings or feelings that life is not worth living.

- Dysthymic disorder is characterized by chronic, persistent, lower-level depressive symptoms that occur over a longer period of time (2 years or longer).

- The bipolar spectrum mood disorders (i.e. bipolar I, bipolar II, cyclothymia) are differentiated from major depressive disorder and dysthymic disorder in that individuals also experience what are called hypomanic or manic episodes. Hypomanic or manic episodes include periods of extreme euphoria—feeling excessively high without the use of a substance. In some cases patients experience this high as an increase in irritability rather than an increase in euphoria. The word *bipolar* is used because individuals experience two emotional extremes—depressed mood and at other times excessive euphoria. Individuals with bipolar I experience full manic episodes; those with bipolar II experience hypomanic episodes—episodes that are not as severe as manic episodes; and those with cyclothymia experience a mix of low-level depressive episodes and hypomanic episodes.

This workbook is designed for individuals with "unipolar" depression: major depression or dysthymia. However, in our clinic and in the studies of this intervention to date, we have included individuals with bipolar disorder who were currently depressed and who had not recently experienced a manic or hypomanic episode. We believe that this workbook would be appropriate for those with bipolar depression if their current major symptom is depression and if their hypomanic or manic episodes are stabilized on medications. Also, although we have designed this workbook for use with clients who have symptoms of depression that are severe enough to warrant a clinical diagnosis, there is evidence that lower levels of depressive symptoms also negatively impact self-care and medication adherence. It is likely that the strategies presented in this workbook could be modified for use with patients who have some symptoms of depression, even if they do not meet criteria for a formal diagnosis.

Why Do Depression and Chronic Medical Illness Overlap?

There are many potential reasons for the overlap between depression and chronic illness. Living with a chronic illness can be stressful and can limit your involvement in things that you previously liked to do. Not having enough enjoyable activities can lead to or maintain symptoms of depression. Further, physical symptoms such as fatigue can impair your ability to keep up with your usual activities. Adjusting to an illness that has waxing and waning symptoms can also be upsetting. Reducing enjoyable activities because of chronic illness can also negatively affect important relationships with friends and family, and this can lead to more feelings of loneliness and depression. Withdrawing from social relationships is one of the common consequences of depression, and it also makes depression worse.

In some cases, the relationship between depression and chronic illness may even be a cycle. In diabetes, for example, depressive symptoms such as reduced energy, lower motivation, and difficulties with problem solving negatively impact self-treatment and can lead to hyperglycemia or high blood sugar. In turn, high blood sugar and the threat of complications can lead to hopelessness, self-blame, and helplessness. In HIV, depression can lead to worse immune functioning, both through worse treatment adherence and possibly through biochemical changes associated with depression. Having worse immune functioning leaves one at risk for various infections, causing symptoms and impairment and consequently leading back to increased depression. Successful treatment may require both decreasing depression *and* improving self-care.

Development of This Treatment Program and Evidence Base

To be considered "valid," psychological treatments require an evidence base. This evidence base is established by research studies that demonstrate the effectiveness of the treatment in a sample of individuals taken from a given population. The evidence base of this approach comes from several sources.

First, many studies of cognitive-behavioral therapy for depression have been done with nonmedical populations. Over the past 30 years, research has consistently validated CBT as a successful treatment for depression, with many studies showing effects similar to or greater than those for medications. Cognitive-behavioral therapy has also been shown to have additional effects for residual symptoms of depression not fully treated by medications alone. CBT is often used to treat patients with depression as an alternative to treatment with medication, and it is also used as an additional component of treatment for patients who are already taking antidepressants.

Second, there are emerging studies of CBT approaches for depression in individuals with chronic medical conditions, particularly HIV and diabetes. Whereas our approach integrates CBT for depression with approaches for improving adherence to medical recommendations, others have studied cognitive-behavioral therapy and cognitive-behavioral stress management for depression in the context of medical illness without specifically addressing the issue of adherence.

Third, the evidence base is supported by our research on a cognitive-behavioral adherence intervention (module 2 in this manual), which has been shown to be effective for improving medication adherence. Finally, we have completed several studies of the specific treatment described in this manual, targeting individuals with HIV and depression. At the time of writing, we are conducting ongoing evaluations of the approach for patients with HIV and for patients with type 2 diabetes.

Risks and Benefits of This Treatment Program

There are no known medical risks to participating in this program. Cognitive-behavioral therapy is a directive, skills-based treatment that focuses on strategies that are designed to directly improve the symptoms of depression. However, as with all treatments, there is always the risk that it will not work. In this case, clients may feel sad, upset, or even hopeless about their depression continuing. We encourage you to discuss this risk with your therapist, to explore reasons for potential treatment nonresponse, and to consider alternative treatments, if necessary.

There are many potential benefits to the treatment program. Depression is a distressing, disabling, and interfering condition that can negatively impact quality of life. Improving depression can improve functioning and well-being. In the context of chronic illness, improving depression may have additional important benefits. Specific symptoms of depression (e.g., poor concentration, loss of interest) or associated symptoms (e.g., low motivation, poor problem solving) can certainly interfere with a person's ability to adhere to a regimen of treatment for a chronic illness. With HIV, for example, adherence to medications is critical for treatment success. With diabetes, adherence to glucose monitoring, insulin and/or medications, exercise recommendations, and a healthy diet can prevent complications and worse medical outcomes. Depression can get in the way of the behaviors necessary for adherence to these and other chronic illnesses. Many other medical illnesses require strict adherence to self-management regimens, and the approach described in this workbook may be applicable to a wide range of illnesses, particularly when depression is also present. As this program aims to improve both depression and your ability to utilize effective strategies to improve your medical adherence, you may experience both quality-of-life and health benefits.

Alternative Treatments

As far as we know, the program described in this workbook is the only scientifically supported intervention that integrates the treatment of depression with a psychosocial approach to improving medical adherence. An alternative treatment for depression only, which has also been proven successful, is interpersonal psychotherapy (IPT). For more information on this therapy, please consult Myrna M. Weissman's *Mastering Depression Through Interpersonal Psychotherapy: Patient Workbook* (Oxford University Press, 2005). Antidepressant medications also have been validated as effective in treating depression. Standard cognitive-behavioral therapy that does not address adherence training is also an option for the treatment of depression. As discussed previously, CBT has been extensively researched and found to be effective in a variety of populations.

The Role of Medications

A variety of medications are available for the treatment of depression. The program described in this workbook is designed to treat depression, in either individuals on antidepressant medications who still show symptoms or individuals who are not currently on antidepressant medications. Having an approach for those who are already on medications is important because, although medications do work, many studies find that only 50% of patients who are treated with antidepressants alone respond favorably. Of those who do respond, only 50–65% attain remission as opposed to symptom reduction only. Many patients treated with antidepressants have significant symptoms that could be addressed with a psychosocial skills-based approach such as the one presented in this workbook. Studies of our program have included participants who were not taking antidepressants and those who were. Those taking antidepressants were enrolled after they had been stabilized on medications so that we could determine the degree to which improvements from the treatment occur over and above the effects of medications. We believe that this program can be useful for patients who are already taking antidepressants, and we also believe that antidepressants can be a useful adjunct to the treatment, particularly for individuals with severe depression. You should discuss any questions that you have about antidepressants with your doctor.

Outline of This Treatment Program

The main modules for this program are as follows:

1. *Psychoeducation and motivational interviewing.* This session or series of sessions with your therapist is designed to help you understand the rationale behind this program and the particular modules involved, as well as to articulate and hopefully enhance your motivation to participate.

2. *Adherence training (Life-Steps).* This session or series of sessions is designed to help you come up with a workable plan for the steps involved in managing your particular medical regimen. This session does not address depression directly but is a basis for future sessions. Most people find it hard to manage a medical regimen at first, and because of the symptoms of depression, people with depression can have an even harder time.

3. *Activity scheduling.* This session or series of sessions is designed to help you identify enjoyable activities that you can participate in outside of the sessions. Both depression and chronic medical

illnesses can make it harder to participate in these types of activities.

4. *Adaptive thinking (cognitive restructuring).* This session or series of sessions is designed to help you think about situations in a rational way that is maximally helpful to you and to the situation. People suffering from depression often exhibit unrealistic or distorted ways of thinking about themselves and their life situations, because depression can negatively color how people interpret events. Specific patterns of negative thinking will be collaboratively identified and challenged in these sessions.

5. *Problem solving.* This session or series of sessions is designed to help you improve your problem-solving skills by teaching you to break down problems into manageable components, generate lists of potential solutions, and select the best response.

6. *Relaxation training and diaphragmatic breathing.* This session or series of sessions involves learning to breathe in a way that minimizes stress or tension. Additionally, it involves specific training in how to relax your body. This can be helpful both for stress and tension and also for managing symptoms from your illness or side effects of medications.

7. *Review, maintenance, and relapse prevention.* This session or series of sessions is designed to help you transition from weekly therapy sessions to doing these skills on your own.

Structure of This Treatment Program

This treatment program is different from traditional psychotherapy. It is more like taking a course in learning how to cope with the difficulties you are having. Sessions are structured, with each one having a set agenda for you and your therapist to follow. Each of the seven modules described builds on previous modules, and each session begins with an assessment and discussion of depression and medical adherence for the previous week. The skills for coping with depression are integrated with skills for managing your medical illness. You and your therapist will work collaboratively to address your symptoms of depression and problems you may be having in following your medical regimen.

Use of the Workbook

This workbook contains all the necessary forms and worksheets you will need throughout treatment, including self-monitoring sheets you can use to track your depression ratings and medical adherence on a weekly basis. Because you will use these sorts of forms on a regular basis, we have provided you with multiple copies. Other forms that will be completed for homework or as in-session exercises are provided only once. If you find that you need extras, you may make photocopies from the book or download multiples from the Treatments *ThatWork*™ website at http://www.oup.com/us/ttw.

Overview of Adherence Behaviors

As discussed, adherence is the degree to which a patient follows a medical regimen that is collaboratively agreed on with his or her medical provider. Most chronic medical illnesses require long-term treatment adherence behaviors. HIV/AIDS and diabetes are probably the most widely known in terms of the importance of strict adherence. Important aspects of treatment for conditions such as hypertension or high blood pressure, asthma, cardiac disease, organ transplant, hepatitis C, and cancer rely on patients' self-care behaviors and/or behavioral change. Although these examples are some of the most common chronic illnesses that require adherence, there are many others. Most of the techniques in this workbook can be applied across a range of illnesses with co-occurring depression. Symptoms of depression can have a strong negative impact on the motivation and skills needed to maintain strict adherence. Some examples of adherence behaviors for particular illnesses are described here. For almost all of the illnesses described, studies have specifically demonstrated associations between depression and poorer adherence.

HIV/AIDS

Currently, the best available treatment for HIV/AIDS is a combination of medications, called highly active antiretroviral therapy, or HAART. Almost perfect adherence to HAART is required to maximize the chances of treatment success and to minimize the chances of developing medication resistance. This is difficult for patients because many experience immediate and long-term side effects, including fatigue, nausea, diarrhea, insomnia, abnormal fat accumulation, taste alterations, and peripheral neuropathy (damage to the peripheral nervous system). Additionally, HAART needs to be taken in the long term—indefinitely.

To get the full therapeutic benefit of HAART, you may need not only to take a high proportion of total doses but also to give strict and near perfect attention to dosing frequency, timing, and food requirements. Hence, for HIV, this manual mainly addresses adherence to HAART. If HAART is highly potent and adherence is perfect, the ability of the virus to copy itself, or replicate, is theoretically shut off. Accordingly, in this case, copies that are resistant to medications do not arise. This makes a patient's viral load (the amount of virus in the bloodstream) go to very low, or even to undetectable, levels (by some instruments). This is called "viral suppression" and is an indication of treatment success. When this happens, the virus is no longer attacking a person's immune system—and this can allow the person's CD4 cell counts (immune cells) to increase, thus making the immune system less vulnerable to infections.

Diabetes

The treatment of diabetes, whether type 1 or 2, depends to a large extent on the patient's self-management. In contrast to HIV, in which medication adherence is the predominant self-care behavior, diabetes requires many self-care behaviors. The treatment of diabetes is therefore sometimes referred to as "lifestyle management."

Both type 1 and type 2 diabetes increase a patient's risk for many serious complications, including cardiovascular disease, retinopathy (noninflammatory damage to the retina of the eye), neuropathy (nerve damage), and nephropathy (kidney damage). The relative risk for these complications depends to a large extent on how well diabetes is controlled over time. In fact, it is estimated that more than 95% of diabetes care consists of self-care behaviors.

Nonadherence can lead to worse control over blood sugar levels (glycemic control) and worse blood pressure and lipid levels, which can result in increased rates of both microvascular complications, such as eye and kidney disease and nerve damage, and macrovascular complications, such as cardiovascular disease. Vascular and nerve damage combine to increase the risk of gangrene, which, in turn, can lead to amputation of lower limbs, reduced life expectancy, and overall poor quality of life. Adherence behaviors involved in the treatment of diabetes can include (1) self-monitoring of blood glucose and making changes based on the results; (2) adhering to medications, possibly including exogenous insulin, to control hyperglycemia, hypertension, and hyperlipidemia; (3) diet, exercise, and other self-care behaviors (e.g., foot care, checking for ulcers, smoking cessation, routine screening for complications, consistent attendance at medical visits).

Hypertension

Hypertension, or high blood pressure, is a very common disorder that places patients at increased risk of stroke, heart attack, congestive heart failure, kidney failure, and peripheral vascular disease. Treatment and the accompanying adherence behaviors required for hypertension depend on the severity of the elevation in blood pressure and the presence of other conditions, such as diabetes. For less severe hypertension, recommended lifestyle changes include losing weight, increasing activity, and eating a balanced diet. For more severe hypertension, prescribed medications are used in conjunction with lifestyle changes. Although pharmacotherapy to reduce hypertension has been proven to be effective, adequate control remains challenging; only one-quarter of patients achieve adequate control. This low level of treatment success is thought to be largely a result of medication nonadherence. Good adherence to medication has been associated with improved blood pressure control and reduced complications of hypertension.

In addition to adherence to medications, lifestyle factors are also important in the management of hypertension. Increasing physical activity and/or aerobic exercise, losing weight, restricting sodium intake, and moderating alcohol intake may all be important self-management goals for patients with hypertension. Proper adherence can help avoid risks of stroke, myocardial infarction (heart attack), congestive heart failure, kidney failure, and peripheral vascular disease. There is some evidence that depression is more common among patients with hypertension and that it can negatively affect adherence to treatment.

Coronary Heart Disease

Recommendations for the treatment of coronary heart disease (CHD) include lifestyle changes (increasing physical activity, losing weight, making dietary changes) and medication regimens. These lifestyle behaviors are similar to the ones described for diabetes and hypertension. Additionally, medications may include high blood pressure medications, medications for cholesterol, and aspirin. Some people may also take medications that control heart rate (i.e., beta-blockers). CHD is a very common disorder that results in significant medical costs, frequent illness episodes, and premature loss of life.

Depression and nonadherence are two related psychosocial factors that have been extensively researched in CHD and that are each associated with poorer health outcomes. For example, patients who have recently had a heart attack, or myocardial infarction (MI), and who report significant symptoms of depression have been found to be more than twice as likely to have a new cardiovascular attack than patients who don't report depression after having an MI. Additionally, data from patients recovering from MI suggest that depression negatively impacts self-care and adherence following discharge. Patients who had had an acute MI in the previous 3 to 5 days and who had symptoms of at least mild to moderate depression were less likely to follow a low-fat diet, to get regular exercise, to reduce stress, and to increase their social support 4 months later. Those with clinical depression also reported taking medications as prescribed less often than those without major depression and/or dysthymia. Nonadherence to these recommendations has been found to be associated with worse outcomes and increased likelihood of death in patients with CHD. Therefore, it is possible that the relationship between depression and worse health outcomes in patients with CHD could be at least partly explained by associated medical nonadherence.

Asthma

Asthma is a chronic disease that involves inflammation of the airways superimposed with recurrent episodes of limited airflow, mucus production, and cough. Asthma is generally diagnosed by periodic symptoms of wheezing, nocturnal awakening from asthma, cough, difficulty breathing, chest tightness, and episodic decreases and variability in pulmonary function. Although effective treatments, which have been shown to dramatically reduce illness severity, are available, nonadherence to these treatments is a widespread problem among patients.

Treatment of asthma involves taking two types of medications aimed at the two components of asthma: airway inflammation and acute bronchoconstriction. Additional adherence behaviors include avoiding things that trigger attacks and self-monitoring symptoms and lung functioning. Corticosteroids are a commonly used anti-inflammatory medication for people suffering from asthma. These and other anti-inflammatory drugs reduce swelling and mucus production in the airways and are usually prescribed to be taken daily. Anti-inflammatory medications control inflammation and prevent chronic symptoms such as coughing or breathlessness at night, in the early morning, or after exertion. Quick-relief medications are also used in the treatment of asthma attack symptoms (cough, chest tightness, and wheezing) when attacks occur. Avoiding asthma triggers such as inhaled allergens and certain foods and medications, irritants such as tobacco smoke, and other triggers is also important. Lastly, self-monitoring of daily asthma symptoms and peak airflow with a flow meter and recording information in a diary is another important aspect of self-management.

The experience of attacks with little apparent warning may encourage patients to think of asthma as a series of unexpected, acute episodes separated by "disease-free" periods. In fact, patients may think, "no symptoms = no asthma," and this type of belief has been found to be associated with inaccurate understanding of asthma and with one-third lower odds of adherence to inhaled corticosteroids during times when patients have no symptoms. Part of adherence to asthma regimens involves making sure that you understand that it is a chronic condition. Self-care behaviors are important even when you are having few symptoms or are relatively symptom free in order to reduce the likelihood that you will have attacks in the future.

Several studies have reported associations between depressive disorders and anxiety disorders and worse asthma control and quality of life. For example, among asthma patients recently discharged from hospitalization, symptoms of depression were found to be quite common, and high levels of depressive symptoms were shown to predict worse adherence to therapy after discharge. For some people, depression can interfere with adherence to asthma treatment.

Hepatitis C Virus (HCV)

Hepatitis C (HCV) is a viral infection that affects the functioning of the liver. Between 15 and 45% of persons with acute hepatitis C will recover, are not at risk of long-term complications, and do not need treatment. However, patients with chronic HCV face a life-threatening illness. The progression to cirrhosis of the liver is the primary concern, although the rate of progression is usually slow, often taking more than two decades. Progression tends to be more common among persons infected at older ages, particularly men; those who drink more than 50 grams of alcohol each day; those who are obese or have substantial hepatic steatosis (accumulation of fat in liver cells); or those who also have HIV infection. The goal of HCV treatment is to eradicate the virus and thus avoid long-term complications of chronic HCV. The most effective current combination treatment available consists of weekly injections under the skin of long-acting peginterferon alfa and oral ribavirin, usually taken over a period of at least 48 weeks. Approximately 46 to 77% of patients achieve a successful response after 48 weeks of combination therapy at the maximal doses.

Although effective, combination therapy commonly causes side effects, including fatigue, influenza-like symptoms, gastrointestinal disturbances, neuropsychiatric symptoms (especially depression), and blood abnormalities. Approximately 75% of treated patients experience one or more side effects of combination therapy, and these side effects may require dose reduction or drug discontinuation. Many patients with HCV discontinue or do not adhere to treatment because of these side effects. Estimates suggest that between 23 and

40% of patients treated for HCV will develop major depression during therapy; furthermore, combination therapy can actually induce depression. There is, however, preliminary evidence that integrating mental health care (including cognitive-behavioral therapy) with medical care in the treatment of patients with chronic HCV can improve adherence to therapy.

Cancer

The availability of oral chemotherapies promises to have a significant impact on the treatment of various forms of cancer in the future. Several oral chemotherapy medications have already become available, and many more are being evaluated in efficacy research trials. Although these oral medications offer significant advantages over standard intravenous treatments, including greater convenience and shorter treatment time, they also require patients to monitor themselves for side effects, and their effects depend on patient adherence to prescribed regimens. Also, because therapy can be self-administered, the patient's contact with health care providers decreases. Although cancer patients may be thought to be highly motivated to adhere to therapy because of the gravity of their disease, nonadherence rates of 43 to 50%, respectively, have been reported in samples of patients with breast cancer and blood malignancies who take oral medications.

Summary

In general, depression is a common condition that occurs along with medical illness. Depression in and of itself is a distressing and interfering condition. In addition, the primary and associated symptoms of depression can dramatically affect the self-care behaviors you need to maintain a medical treatment regimen. Integrating CBT for depression with adherence-promoting interventions can have significant impacts on your quality of life and physical health while you are managing a chronic illness. We describe this intervention in the forthcoming chapters.

Chapter 2

Overview of the Program

Goals

- To learn about depression in the context of having a chronic illness

- To understand the three components of depression and how they interact

- To introduce the cognitive-behavioral model of depression and understand how it applies to you

- To learn about this treatment program and what it will involve

Depression and Chronic Illness

Many people who live with a chronic medical illness such as cancer, diabetes, high blood pressure, asthma, or HIV also suffer from depression. Some data suggest that up to 30% of individuals with a medical condition experience depression and that depression is the most common condition that co-occurs with a medical illness. Depression is a significant and impairing disorder for individuals with a chronic medical condition. It has been shown that depressed individuals who suffer from a chronic illness experience greater distress and more medical problems and complications than those individuals who are chronically ill but not depressed. Depression can impact your ability to perform important self-care behaviors, including following your prescribed medical regimen, whether it includes taking regular doses of medication or improving your eating and exercise habits. In fact, individuals with depression are three times more likely than nondepressed individuals to be nonadherent to medical treatment recommendations. This program is specifically designed to help you overcome your depression so you can take better care of yourself and manage your illness.

To understand the treatment approach described in this manual, it is important to understand the cognitive, behavioral, and physical components that make up depression and how they can relate to your illness. Although this type of treatment has been helpful for many people with depression, fighting depression is not an easy task. Understanding the different components of depression will greatly help you understand the rationale behind the coping techniques outlined in this workbook.

Cognitive Component

The cognitive component of depression consists of the negative thoughts that you have when you are depressed. When people are depressed, they tend to look at themselves, their world, and their future more negatively than when they are not depressed. These negative thoughts can involve negative beliefs about your ability to cope (e.g., "There is no way I can manage everything I need to for this illness"), excessive and unwarranted self-blame (e.g., "This illness is some kind of punishment for bad things I have done"), or other negative thoughts about yourself (e.g., "I am unlovable because of this illness and how I am managing it").

Behavioral Component

The behavioral component of depression refers to the particular behaviors that you do or don't do because you are depressed, including avoiding activities that normally provide you enjoyment. These types of behaviors can increase your depression significantly and can decrease your motivation to take care of yourself and follow the recommendations of your doctor or medical team.

According to the cognitive-behavioral model of depression, the behavioral components of depression are directly related to the cognitive components. A depressed individual with a chronic medical condition may be more likely to think a thought such as "There is no way I can manage my illness." If someone with depression is thinking a thought like this, he or she may be much less likely to actively try to manage the illness because he or she does not believe that he or she can do it. When a depressed person "gives up" or does not make the effort to manage his or her illness, he or she will not succeed at managing the illness, and then the strength of the negative thought, "There is no way I can manage my illness," is increased. So, because negative thoughts influence our behavior, they can "snowball" over time and become stronger as they collect more and more evidence supporting the original belief. Often, the person experiencing the thought is unaware that this negative thought is influencing his or her behavior and thus fails to see that he or she is caught in this cycle. Negative thoughts can thus result in "self-fulfilling prophecies." We make a negative prediction about the future, and then we act in ways that ensure that the prediction will come true. For example, a person might have the negative thought, "I'll never find anyone who will love me." In response to this thought the person might decide that there's no point in trying to meet anyone and may withdraw from others and from social activities. As a result, the person may indeed end up spending much of his or her time alone because he or she is not taking any steps to make it possible to meet someone. In the end it may seem that the thought was accurate, but this happens only because the behavioral response (isolating and withdrawing) created a situation in which only evidence that supported the thought (e.g., not meeting anyone, spending the weekends alone at home) could be gathered. Thus our negative thoughts, which are often inaccurate, can have a powerful effect on our behaviors. The maladaptive behaviors (e.g., withdrawing, isolating, giving up pleasurable activities), which are driven by negative thoughts, can cause a person to become depressed and can maintain the depression once it begins.

Physiological Component

The physiological (or physical) component of depression can be complex in individuals with chronic illnesses. The reason is that physical symptoms of the illness can be similar to physical symptoms of depression. A person who does not have a chronic illness but does have depression may have such physical symptoms of depression as low energy, decreased appetite, fatigue, sleep problems, and poor concentration. These symptoms can be exacerbated by chronic illness and/or medications and therefore also affect adherence.

The physical component of depression is also related to the cognitive and behavioral components, creating a cycle. For example, if someone is feeling tired, either due to depression itself, to complications of a medical illness, or to symptoms from side effects of medications, this will affect his or her ability and motivation to engage in enjoyable events. This then can be associated with the cognitive component of depression, as depicted earlier. Additionally, physical symptoms of depression or a chronic medical illness can be directly associated with the cognitive component of depression. For example, someone who is feeling tired may be more likely to think "I can't do this because of my symptoms." Hence there is a cycle between the cognitive, behavioral, and physical symptoms of depression that can be exacerbated by symptoms of a chronic medical illness.

Your Model of Depression

Your therapist will work with you to complete the cognitive-behavioral model of depression as it specifically applies to you. This model will show you how your behaviors and thoughts and the physical effects of your illness interact with one another and can maintain your depression. You and your therapist can use the questions that follow, as well as additional discussion, to record your specific symptoms for each category in the blank model shown in figure 2.1.

Your Thoughts

- What is your thinking like since you have become depressed?

- What thoughts do you have about yourself? Your relationships with others? Your future? Your illness? Your treatment? Your medications?

Your Behaviors

- What types of things do you think you avoid or do less often because you are depressed?

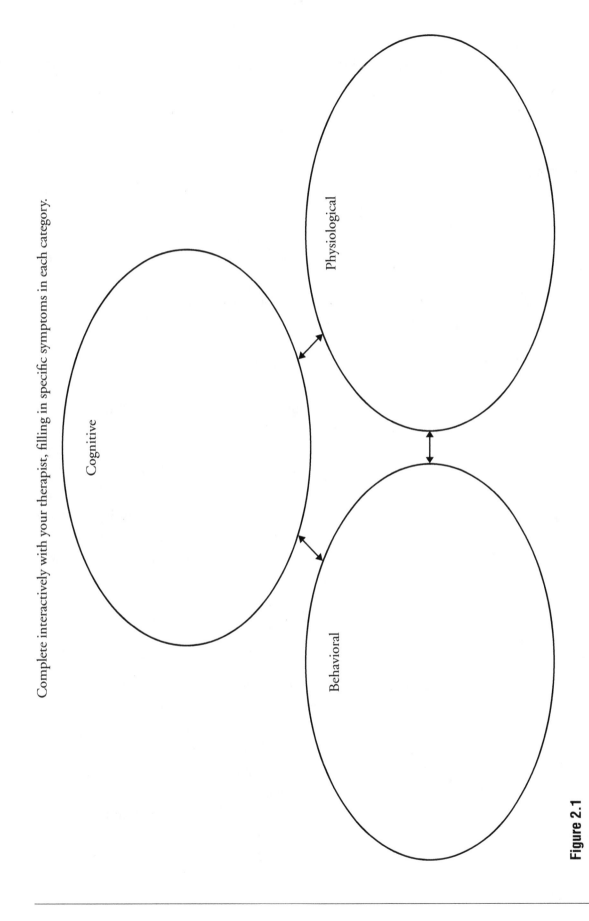

Complete interactively with your therapist, filling in specific symptoms in each category.

Cognitive

Physiological

Behavioral

Figure 2.1

Cognitive–Behavioral Model of Depression

> What kinds of things do you do more of because you are depressed?

> How have your relationships changed since you have become depressed?

Your Symptoms

> What physical symptoms do you experience?

> Do you have trouble sleeping? Trouble concentrating?

> Do you experience changes in your appetite?

> Are you fatigued? Do you lack energy?

The Cycle of Depression

As illustrated by your model, depression is a cycle. When you have negative thoughts going through your head, you are less likely to engage in pleasurable activities and more likely to withdraw from others. When you are isolated you are more likely to feel fatigued and less energetic. Because you are tired and lethargic, you will feel more depressed. This leads to more negative thoughts, causing the whole cycle to start over again. This treatment program is designed to help you break the cycle of depression. It is meant to be completed with the assistance of a cognitive-behavioral therapist.

Focus of Treatment

The main goals of this treatment are to attack each of the three components of depression and to break the connections between them, which will help you better manage your chronic illness. This program consists of modules that teach you skills to attack the components of depression while helping you improve your medical adherence. Unlike traditional psychotherapy, which is open ended, this treatment program is structured. It is like taking a course. Each module consists of a session or sessions, and each session has an agenda. You and your therapist will set the agenda at the start of every meeting. It is important to do your best to stick to the agenda. Following is a summary of each of the modules in this program.

As briefly discussed in the previous chapter, this program contains seven modules. Here, we list them sequentially and provide more detail. Depending on what you and your therapist decide, you may complete the modules in a different order than outlined here and you may focus more or less time on each one.

Life-Steps

The Life-Steps module is an intervention designed to teach you the skills you need to better manage your illness. You will learn how to use problem-solving skills to identify strategies for getting to your medical appointments on time, for communicating with your doctor, and for remembering to take your medication, among other things. This module does not directly deal with depression, but future modules that do deal with depression integrate materials from this module.

Activity Scheduling

This module will address the behavioral component of your depression. Remember, this refers to the behaviors you do or don't do because you are depressed or that you do less of due to your chronic illness. If you are no longer participating in activities that provide you with pleasure, this module will help you get reinvolved in activities and events to help improve your mood. Some people find that when they are depressed, they avoid others and isolate themselves. This module will help you to avoid doing this. Additionally, you will learn how to monitor your activities and your mood, which will help you pace yourself. Given that a chronic medical illness may have symptoms that wax and wane, one goal of this module is for you to learn, through experience, what your limits are and to allow yourself to set and achieve attainable goals for involvement in activities.

Cognitive Restructuring or Adaptive Thinking

This module deals directly with the cognitive component of depression. It describes strategies for attacking thinking that is excessively negative, inaccurate, or counterproductive. You will learn how to challenge your negative thoughts and develop more adaptive, balanced, and realistic ways of thinking.

Problem Solving

Many people with a chronic illness and many people with depression become overwhelmed when confronted with certain problems. The problem-solving module is focused on two concrete skills to help people problem-solve. These skills are selecting an action plan and breaking overwhelming problems into manageable steps. This module includes both cognitive and behavioral components.

Relaxation Training and Diaphragmatic Breathing

Relaxation training can help people with symptoms related to stress. Again, this stress can be due to depression and/or to medical illness. Some people find relaxation training helpful in alleviating symptoms of fatigue, lack of energy, and problems with sleep. Others find that it can help cope with physical symptoms caused by illness, such as side effects of medications, headaches, or pain. This module describes a procedure called progressive muscle relaxation (PMR) and also provides training in breathing in a way that increases feelings of relaxation and decreases tension.

Review, Maintenance, and Relapse Prevention

This final module of the program will help you prepare for the end of treatment and help you transition to becoming your own therapist. This treatment is not necessarily meant to be ongoing. The goal is for you to learn these skills and apply them to your life. This module will assist in transitioning you out of active treatment with a therapist into continued active use of the various skills you learned through working with your therapist.

Each session covers new material and reviews material presented in previous sessions to ensure that you continue to build on prior learning.

Format of Treatment

Each session with your therapist will follow a specific format, as outlined here.

Setting an Agenda

Your therapist will start each session by setting an agenda. This helps maintain a structured focus of the treatment on depression and medical adherence and also prepares you for what lies ahead in upcoming sessions.

Review of Progress

At the start of every session, your therapist will ask you to complete the Center for Epidemiologic Studies Depression Scale (CES-D). The CES-D is a 20-item self-report measure of depression. We have provided a copy for you here and at the start of every chapter beginning in chapter 3. You will complete this self-report every week. If you need additional copies, you may photocopy the measure from the book or download multiples from the Treatments *ThatWork*™ website at http://www.oup.com/us/ttw.

You are asked to rate how each of the 20 items on the CES-D has applied to you over the past week, using a 0- to 3-point scale where 0 = *rarely or none of the time,* 1 = *some or a little of the time,* 2 = *occasionally or a moderate amount of the time,* and 3 = *most or all of the time.* The CES-D is scored by adding up all of the items. A score of 16 or higher suggests clinically significant levels of depression. The higher your score, the more likely it is that you meet the criteria for depression.

In addition to completing the CES-D at every session, your therapist will ask you to fill out the Weekly Adherence Assessment Form. Starting at the next session, you will use this form to assess any medical changes you experienced over the past week, including changes in symptoms or the emergence of new ones. Your therapist will discuss the relation of these medical changes to your adherence behavior and your overall mood.

Center for Epidemiologic Studies Depression Scale (CES-D)

Below is a list of the ways you might have felt or behaved. Please tell me how often you have felt this way during the past week.

	During the Past Week			
	Rarely or none of the time (less than 1 day)	Some or a little of the time (1–2 Days)	Occasionally or a moderate amount of time (3–4 days)	Most or all of the time (5–7 days)
1. I was bothered by things that usually don't bother me.	☐	☐	☐	☐
2. I did not feel like eating; my appetite was poor.	☐	☐	☐	☐
3. I felt that I could not shake off the blues even with help from my family or friends.	☐	☐	☐	☐
4. I felt I was just as good as other people.	☐	☐	☐	☐
5. I had trouble keeping my mind on what I was doing.	☐	☐	☐	☐
6. I felt depressed.	☐	☐	☐	☐
7. I felt that everything I did was an effort.	☐	☐	☐	☐
8. I felt hopeful about the future.	☐	☐	☐	☐
9. I thought my life had been a failure.	☐	☐	☐	☐
10. I felt fearful.	☐	☐	☐	☐
11. My sleep was restless.	☐	☐	☐	☐
12. I was happy.	☐	☐	☐	☐
13. I talked less than usual.	☐	☐	☐	☐
14. I felt lonely.	☐	☐	☐	☐
15. People were unfriendly.	☐	☐	☐	☐
16. I enjoyed life.	☐	☐	☐	☐
17. I had crying spells.	☐	☐	☐	☐
18. I felt sad.	☐	☐	☐	☐
19. I felt that people dislike me.	☐	☐	☐	☐
20. I could not get "going."	☐	☐	☐	☐

SCORING: zero for answers in the first column, 1 for answers in the second column, 2 for answers in the third colomn, 3 for answers in the fourth column. The scoring of positive items is reversed. Possible range of scores is zero to 60, with the higher scores indicating the presence of more symptomatology.

As with the CES-D, we include a copy of the Weekly Adherence Assessment here, as well as at the start of every chapter beginning in chapter 3. If you need additional copies, you may photocopy the form from the book or download multiples from the Treatments *ThatWork*™ website at http://www.oup.com/us/ttw.

We also include, at the end of this chapter, a copy of the Progress Summary Chart for you to record and monitor your progress in treatment. This form allows you to keep track of the degree to which the skills you are learning are actually helping with your depression and your adherence to your medical regimen. Complete this form on a weekly basis, as you will review its contents at every session with your therapist.

Review of Previous Material and Homework

At every session, your therapist will review with you the content of your last session and address any questions or concerns you may have. He or she will also review your completed homework assignment. We have provided a checklist for monitoring your homework assignments at the end of the chapter. This checklist can be used on a week-to-week basis in order to see what strategies are working and which ones aren't. Although the checklist is in the order in which the modules are presented in the workbook, you and your therapist may complete certain modules, and therefore certain homework exercises, in a different order—so some will not apply on certain weeks.

Homework

At the end of every session your therapist will work with you to come up with homework exercises based on the skills taught during treatment. Probably the biggest part of cognitive behavioral treatments in general and this treatment in particular is the emphasis on what you do outside of the sessions—that you learn to apply these strategies to your life. It is important that you understand the rationale behind the various homework assignments, as well as what is being asked of you. As previously stated, homework will be reviewed at the start of every session, so it is important that you do your best to complete your assignments and bring them with you. It's also important

Weekly Adherence Assessment Form

You will complete this form at the start of every session. You will work with your therapist to determine your adherence goals during the Life-Steps intervention (module 2) of this treatment program.

Thinking about the **PAST WEEK**, on average how would you rate your ability to adhere to your goal of

_____?

(Check one)

Very poor	Poor	Fair	Good	Very good	Excellent
☐	☐	☐	☐	☐	☐

Thinking about the **PAST WEEK**, on average how would you rate your ability to adhere to your goal of

_____?

(Check one)

Very poor	Poor	Fair	Good	Very good	Excellent
☐	☐	☐	☐	☐	☐

Thinking about the **PAST WEEK**, on average how would you rate your ability to adhere to your goal of

_____?

(Check one)

Very poor	Poor	Fair	Good	Very good	Excellent
☐	☐	☐	☐	☐	☐

Thinking about the **PAST WEEK**, on average how would you rate your ability to adhere to your goal of

_____?

(Check one)

Very poor	Poor	Fair	Good	Very good	Excellent
☐	☐	☐	☐	☐	☐

for you to remember that although we refer to these out-of-session exercises as "homework," this is not like the homework you used to do in school. You are not going to be graded, and there is no right or wrong way to complete an assignment. The importance of these homework exercises is to allow you to have opportunities to test out some of the skills and ideas that you learn in your sessions in real time. Experiential learning is a very effective strategy, and nothing beats the opportunity to try these skills out in a variety of situations in your own life. You may only see your therapist for 1 hour per week, but there are many other hours in your week available to you for collecting information and testing out your new skills. Making the most of this time in between sessions is essential in order for you to have a good chance at improving your depression. Even when homework exercises don't go well, they provide important information for you and your therapist to consider together in your next session.

Your Goals for Participating in the Program

Your therapist will want to talk to you about your reasons for wanting to participate in this treatment program. Because treatment involves behavioral change, it is important that you understand and discuss with your therapist the various pros and cons of this program. This conversation, in part, is an informed-consent process and in part a way of gauging and enhancing your motivation to try new strategies, which will hopefully be helpful to you.

Understanding your motivation is important in this type of treatment because of the need to make changes outside of the sessions. As with any behavioral-change program, it is important for you to be able to make informed decisions about the degree to which you will use any new strategy. This is the reason we have you monitor the strategies you use, as well as the results you get from them. Remember, if there is any new strategy that you and your therapist talk about that does not work for you or is too difficult, you can always go back to your old way of coping. The goal here, however, is to try some new strategies and see if they are helpful.

What is your general motivation? Review your model of depression and the problem areas you identified and complete the motivational exercise that follows.

Motivational Exercise

Use the form provided to determine the pros and cons of changing, as well as the pros and cons of not changing. Note that there are spaces for both the pros of changing and the cons of not changing, as well as the cons of changing and the pros of not changing. We have found that although some of the boxes are similar (i.e., pros of changing may be similar to cons of not changing), carefully thinking through each can yield additional answers that clients may not have been aware of at first. It is important to emphasize that there are definitely pros of not changing—that people are used to the way things are now, and not changing may be more comfortable and may be, in some ways, easier in the short term. The cons of not changing, however, can mean that you do not get a chance to see whether some of these strategies will actually make a difference and thereby improve your quality of life.

After completing this exercise interactively with your therapist, rate your level of motivation on a scale of 1–10, with 1 representing no motivation at all and 10 representing high motivation.

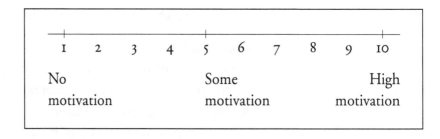

Motivational Exercise: Pros and Cons of Changing

	Pros	Cons
Changing Working to improve depression		
Not changing Keeping things the way they are		

Progress Summary Chart

Date	Module Covered	CES-D Score	Adherence Rating	Homework Assigned	Past Week's Homework Rating

Homework Rating Chart

Instructions: Please rate your practice of the following skills for depression treatment since your last session. Place a check in the column if you tried this skill. Only mark skills that you and your therapist discussed, because your therapist may go through modules in a different order from how they're presented in this manual. Also, it is useful to jot down some notes about your practice so that you can discuss this with your therapist. This can be done in the right-hand column.

Skills	✓	Notes About Your Homework Practice
Activity Scheduling Monitor activities and mood on a daily basis using Activity Log Incorporate activities that involve pleasure or mastery into daily schedule		
Cognitive Restructuring (Adaptive Thinking) Identify automatic thoughts Identify cognitive distortions Record automatic thoughts and match to distortions using Thought Record Challenge automatic thoughts and come up with a rational response		
Problem Solving Practice problem-solving strategies (articulate the problem, generate possible solutions, choose the best alternative) Break tasks down into manageable steps		
Relaxation Training Diaphragmatic breathing Progressive muscle relaxation		

Chapter 3   *Life-Steps*

Goals

- To continue monitoring your progress using the CES-D and Weekly Adherence Assessment Form

- To learn skills for managing your medical routine and self-care behaviors

- To use problem-solving techniques to work out any problems you may have with medical adherence

- To identify exercises for home practice

Review of Depression Scale

Complete the CES-D and review your score with your therapist. Take note of symptoms that have improved and those that are still problematic. Be sure to record your score on the Progress Summary Chart provided in the previous chapter.

Review of Weekly Adherence Assessment

Use the Weekly Adherence Assessment Form to record any medical changes you have experienced since the last session, including changes in your symptoms, emergence of new ones, and any new test results. Rate your adherence and record it on the Progress Summary Chart.

Center for Epidemiologic Studies Depression Scale (CES-D)

Below is a list of the ways you might have felt or behaved. Please tell me how often you have felt this way during the past week.

	During the Past Week			
	Rarely or none of the time (less than 1 day)	Some or a little of the time (1–2 Days)	Occasionally or a moderate amount of time (3–4 days)	Most or all of the time (5–7 days)
1. I was bothered by things that usually don't bother me.	☐	☐	☐	☐
2. I did not feel like eating; my appetite was poor.	☐	☐	☐	☐
3. I felt that I could not shake off the blues even with help from my family or friends.	☐	☐	☐	☐
4. I felt I was just as good as other people.	☐	☐	☐	☐
5. I had trouble keeping my mind on what I was doing.	☐	☐	☐	☐
6. I felt depressed.	☐	☐	☐	☐
7. I felt that everything I did was an effort.	☐	☐	☐	☐
8. I felt hopeful about the future.	☐	☐	☐	☐
9. I thought my life had been a failure.	☐	☐	☐	☐
10. I felt fearful.	☐	☐	☐	☐
11. My sleep was restless.	☐	☐	☐	☐
12. I was happy.	☐	☐	☐	☐
13. I talked less than usual.	☐	☐	☐	☐
14. I felt lonely.	☐	☐	☐	☐
15. People were unfriendly.	☐	☐	☐	☐
16. I enjoyed life.	☐	☐	☐	☐
17. I had crying spells.	☐	☐	☐	☐
18. I felt sad.	☐	☐	☐	☐
19. I felt that people dislike me.	☐	☐	☐	☐
20. I could not get "going."	☐	☐	☐	☐

SCORING: zero for answers in the first column, 1 for answers in the second column, 2 for answers in the third colomn, 3 for answers in the fourth column. The scoring of positive items is reversed. Possible range of scores is zero to 60, with the higher scores indicating the presence of more symptomatology.

Weekly Adherence Assessment Form

You will complete this form at the start of every session. You will work with your therapist to determine your adherence goals during the Life-Steps intervention (module 2) of this treatment program.

Thinking about the **PAST WEEK**, on average how would you rate your ability to adhere to your goal of

?

(Check one)

Very poor	Poor	Fair	Good	Very good	Excellent
☐	☐	☐	☐	☐	☐

Thinking about the **PAST WEEK**, on average how would you rate your ability to adhere to your goal of

?

(Check one)

Very poor	Poor	Fair	Good	Very good	Excellent
☐	☐	☐	☐	☐	☐

Thinking about the **PAST WEEK**, on average how would you rate your ability to adhere to your goal of

?

(Check one)

Very poor	Poor	Fair	Good	Very good	Excellent
☐	☐	☐	☐	☐	☐

Thinking about the **PAST WEEK**, on average how would you rate your ability to adhere to your goal of

?

(Check one)

Very poor	Poor	Fair	Good	Very good	Excellent
☐	☐	☐	☐	☐	☐

Review of Previous Module

Each week you should examine your progress in implementing skills from each of the previous modules. It is important to acknowledge the successes you have achieved and to problem-solve around any difficulties.

Last session involved discussion of the cognitive, behavioral, and physical components of depression. Review the personalized model of depression you created and the way each of the three components interact.

Remember, after this session that emphasizes adherence, you will learn skills and strategies to interrupt the cycle of depression. If you have any questions at this point, now is the time to ask your therapist. Today's session does not directly deal with depression but lays the groundwork for future sessions that integrate treating depression with improving or maintaining the degree to which you manage your illness.

Life-Steps: Adherence and Self-Care Enhancement

The purpose of this module is to help you effectively follow the medical regimen prescribed by your doctor or other health care provider. For many people with a chronic medical condition, this involves regular use of medications. For others it also involves other difficult changes, such as following dietary restrictions, increasing exercise, monitoring one's health using blood or other types of biological tests, and maintaining medical or mental health appointments.

In today's session, you and your therapist are going to start by making sure you have all the best skills to help you manage your illness. This is important for two reasons. First, making sure that you're doing everything you can to manage your illness is the best way to keep you physically healthy. Second, if you feel less overwhelmed by your self-care regimen (because you feel that you've developed a plan and have the skills to put that plan into practice), you may also likely feel less depressed.

Self-care behaviors and medical adherence are an important part of the treatment of all chronic illnesses. Sometimes what you do at home and in your day-to-day life to manage your illness has a much bigger impact on your health than what happens in your doctor's office. For example, it's estimated that 95% of successful treatment for individuals with diabetes depends on self-care behaviors. Research has shown that lifestyle changes for diabetes can be just as powerful as medications in preventing complications. For HIV, taking your medications on time as close to every time as possible is the best way to keep your viral load down and your CD4 cells up. For asthma, carrying your inhaler and taking your preventive medications regularly is the best way to avoid serious attacks. So, a lot of managing a chronic illness relies on what you do. That can be stressful for a lot of people, but it's also good news because it means that a good amount of your health is under *your* control. In this program, we want to take as much of the stress of self-care as possible out of the picture and give you the skills necessary for medical adherence so that you can feel in control of your illness.

Many people can feel overwhelmed when first confronted with the number of new things needed to manage a complicated medical regimen. Being able to manage your illness doesn't have anything to do with what kind of person you are. It's something that changes over time and depends on the skills and support you have to successfully carry out your self-care regimen. It can be a lot like learning to drive a car for the first time. First, you need to learn about all the steps and why they're important: how to hold the wheel, how much pressure to apply to the pedals, when to check your mirrors, and so forth. At first, each one of these steps requires a lot of concentration and effort. You have to specifically remember to do them, and make sure to focus your attention. After doing them repeatedly over time, they feel less and less like steps and more and more like automatic behaviors. As much as possible, we want to help you learn the skills necessary to manage your illness well enough so that you can incorporate them into your life in a way that makes them feel almost as automatic as all those steps involved in driving a car. Just as you learn the steps of driving a car because a car can take you places you want to go, learning the steps involved in managing your illness and following through with them is the best way you can get to better health and quality of life.

Part of this process involves the use of problem-solving skills. One part of problem solving involves defining the problem and breaking it down into steps. A future module is dedicated to this general approach, but before that we are going to directly apply problem solving to medical adherence.

In problem solving, the first thing needed is to define the problem and articulate goals. So, that is where we will begin today.

Before we start, what thoughts do you have regarding adherence to your medical regimen (i.e., taking pills, monitoring glucose)?

1. _____

2. _____

3. _____

4. _____

5. _____

What may get in the way of adhering to your regimen (i.e., your schedule, a tendency to forget, negative thoughts, depression, etc.)?

1. _____

2. _____

3. _____

4. _____

5. _____

When you look at your medications and supplies, what goes through your mind?

1. _____

2. _____

3. _____

4. _____

5. _____

What are your top five reasons for staying adherent and taking care of your medical illness?

1. _____

2. _____

3. _____

4. _____

5. _____

Problem-Solving Steps: The AIM Method

We are now going to go through a checklist of problems that some people have with medical adherence. By completing the checklist, solving problems related to adherence, and continuing to practice, you can make successful adherence a part of your routine.

We will use a technique called AIM to solve some of your adherence-related problems.

The first step in AIM is to

▪ Articulate the particular adherence goal.

The second step is to

▪ Identify barriers to reaching the goal.

The final step is to

▪ Make a plan to overcome the barriers, as well as to develop a backup plan.

With the help of your therapist, use the Adherence Goals Worksheet provided to write down the self-care adherence behaviors that are specific to you and your illness. Together, you and your therapist will target these goals and develop plans for meeting them.

Life-Step 1: Getting to Appointments

This first step will help you identify ways that will help you get to your medical appointments.

Adherence Goals Worksheet

Name _____ Date _____

Generate a list of adherence/self-care goals and write them here.

Goal 1: _____

_____

_____

_____

Goal 2: _____

_____

_____

_____

Goal 3: _____

_____

_____

_____

Goal 4: _____

_____

_____

_____

Goal 5: _____

_____

_____

_____

AIM

1. Articulate the adherence goal regarding medical appointments. How often do you have medical appointments? Where are they located?

_____

_____

_____

2. Identify potential barriers. What might cause you to miss appointments? Does your work schedule conflict? Do you live very far away?

_____

_____

_____

3. Make a plan and a backup plan.

Plan: _____

_____

Backup plan: _____

_____

Life-Step 2: Communicating With Treatment Team

Communication with your medical provider can be a key component of treatment success. We have found that many clients have difficulties remembering questions to ask their provider, become nervous during medical visits, and forget information. Developing a plan for enhancing communication with your doctor or medical team can be very helpful.

AIM

1. Articulate any questions or comments that you would like to ask or discuss with your medical provider. What questions do

you want to ask about your symptoms, medications, side effects, or recommended self-care behaviors?

_____

_____

_____

2. Identify potential barriers to communication with your medical provider. Do you feel uncomfortable talking to your doctor? Do you feel that he or she is too busy to talk to you? Do you tend to forget what you want to ask?

_____

_____

_____

3. Make a plan and a backup plan:

Plan: _____

_____

Backup plan: _____

_____

Some people find it helpful to write out all of their questions on a 3 × 5 card, in a notebook, or on a piece of paper to bring with them to their provider visit. This way, not only do you remember the questions to ask but having something written also provides a structure to the questions. For example, you could say to the provider "I have three things I want to ask about and I wrote them down." This way, it sets the expectation that there are three things and the provider is more likely to wait for all three before interrupting or moving on to something else.

Life-Step 3: Coping With Side Effects

If you are taking medication to manage your illness, you are no doubt experiencing some side effects. There are many potential solutions to side effects, but many have remedies that vary across illnesses. Work with your therapist to clearly identify the side effects that you find most distressing and make a plan to talk to your physician about ways to manage them. Additionally, you may be able to find information on coping with side effects on the Internet. Be sure to use reputable sources, however, and don't try anything without consulting your doctor first.

AIM

1. Articulate any problems with adherence that may emerge due to side effects. What kinds of side effects do you experience? Which of your medications do you think are causing the side effects?

   _____

   _____

   _____

2. Identify potential barriers. Have your side effects gotten in the way of your taking your medication? What have you done about the side effects so far? Have you been able to talk to your doctor about them?

   _____

   _____

   _____

3. Make a plan and a backup plan:

   Plan: _____

   _____

   Backup plan: _____

   _____

Life-Step 4: Obtaining Medications and Other Relevant Health-Related Products

We encourage you to work with your provider to develop a plan for continued access to medications or other products (e.g., a glucose monitor if you have diabetes, an inhaler if you have asthma, etc.).

The plan should include information regarding payment options, pharmacy selection, backup plans for transportation or other issues, and management of client-pharmacist transactions.

AIM

1. Articulate the adherence goal of always having a sufficient supply of medications and needed products. Where do you get your medications and medical supplies? How do you pay for them? How do you get to your pharmacy? Have you ever run out of your medications or medical supplies? When do you ask for a medication refill from your pharmacy? When do you ask for a refill from your doctor?

    _____

    _____

    _____

2. Identify potential barriers. What might cause you to run out of your medications or other needed medical supplies? What might get in the way of getting to your pharmacy?

    _____

    _____

    _____

3. Make a plan and a backup plan:

    Plan: _____

    _____

    Backup plan: _____

    _____

Life-Step 5: Formulating a Daily Medication Schedule

This step will help you devise ways of reminding yourself to take your medication. Complete the Medical Regimen Schedule worksheet provided and review and discuss it with your therapist. We

Medical Regimen Schedule

Day of the Week: _Tuesday_

Adherence Goals: _Take all prescribed medications_

Check glucose 3x

Take 2 insulin doses

Increase physical activity

Time	Daily Activity	Adherence Goal
Morning 6:30	Wake up & use bathroom	
7:00	Get dressed	Check glucose level and take insulin
7:30	Eat breakfast	
8:00	Drive to work	Take morning medications
9:00	Arrive at work	
10:00	Work	
11:00	Snack break	
Afternoon 12:00	Work	
1:00	Lunch	Check glucose level after lunch
2:00–4:00	Work	
4:00	Snack break	
5:00	Leave work	
Evening 6:00	Go to gym	Physical activity
7:00	Eat dinner	Take evening medications
8:00–10:00	Watch TV	Take insulin after dinner
10:00	Read the paper	Check glucose level
10:30	Go to bed	

Figure 3.1

Example of Completed Medical Regimen Schedule

Medical Regimen Schedule

Day of the Week: _____

Adherence Goals: _____

_____

_____

_____

Time	Daily Activity	Adherence Goal
Morning		
Afternoon		
Evening		

have provided a sample (figure 3.1) for you to use as a model when filling out your own.

AIM

1. Articulate the adherence goal of remembering to take your medication and follow your medical regimen. When do you take your medications? How do you remember to take your medications? How often do you need to exercise? How often do you need to perform other self-management behaviors (e.g., testing your blood sugar if you are diabetic)?

   _____

   _____

   _____

2. Identify potential barriers. When do you tend to forget to take your medications? Do you usually take your medications when you are doing something else?

   _____

   _____

   _____

3. Make a plan and a backup plan:

   Plan: _____

   _____

   Backup plan: _____

   _____

Life-Step 6: Storing Medications and Medical Supplies

Some medications require safe and portable storage or refrigeration. If this is the case with your medicines, you will work with your therapist to address this issue.

AIM

1. Articulate the adherence goal of properly storing medications, even when you are not at home. If you leave home, do you take your medications with you if you know you will not be back in time for your dose? How do you carry your medications or medical monitoring devices with you when you go out?

    _____

    _____

    _____

2. Identify potential barriers. How do you take your medications with you when you go out? Do any of your medications need to be refrigerated? What will you do about storing medications when you are away from home?

    _____

    _____

    _____

3. Make a plan and a backup plan:

    Plan: _____

    _____

    Backup plan: _____

    _____

Life-Step 7: Cue-Control Strategies for Taking Medications

Your therapist will introduce you to a system for reminding yourself to take your medications. Use round, colored adhesive stickers that you can find in any office supply store and place them in or around your home or workplace as reminder cues. Then take one of the same stickers and place it on a note card. Write on the note card a particular issue you want to be reminded of when you see the stickers elsewhere. For example, you may write, "I am taking my medicine so I can be healthy for my loved ones." Post the note card in a place where you will see it often, so that whenever you see a sticker in your home or at your job, you can remember what it stands for.

AIM

1. Articulate the adherence goal of using strategies for improving your motivation to take medications and for remembering to take them. How do you usually help remind yourself to take your medications? What do you think about when you know it is time to take your medications?

    _____

    _____

    _____

2. Identify potential barriers. What things do you think may keep you from using the dots? Do you think the dots would be helpful reminders to take your medications?

    _____

    _____

    _____

3. Make a plan and a backup plan:

    Plan: _____

    _____

    Backup plan: _____

    _____

Life-Step 8: Handling Slips in Adherence

This step will help you prepare to recover from missing doses, or lapsing from an exercise routine, or breaking your diet regimen, or any other slip-up you may experience related to your medical routine. If a lapse occurs, the best choice is to return to your adherence program as soon as possible instead of acting on hopeless thoughts and giving up. Identifying what led to the lapse can provide you with important information that can help solidify your coping skills and avoid future lapses. Lapses are normal and not a big problem. They only become a big problem when they lead to relapse and cause you to give up on your self-care regimen.

Although you may expect that you will continually improve as your treatment progresses, this may not be the case. Everyone experiences ups and downs and good days and bad days.

Look at the graph in figure 3.2. It shows the difference between what most people who participate in this program believe their progress should look like and the reality of how progress usually happens. At times during your involvement with this program, you may experience a worsening of your symptoms or difficulty using the skills

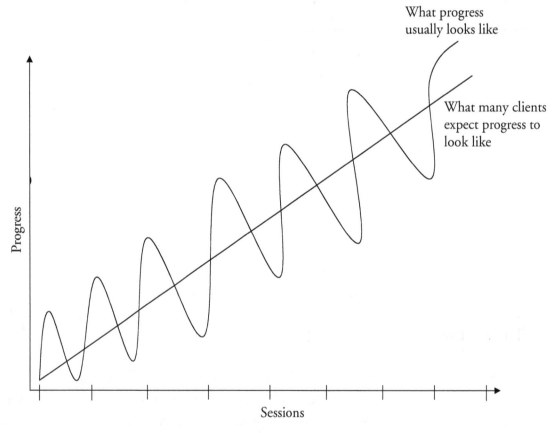

Figure 3.2

Improvement Graph

you've learned effectively. Instead of losing hope, look at these times as opportunities to gather information about what contributed to the negative change and use this knowledge to better prepare yourself in the future. Remember, lapses are completely normal. Over the long run, successfully dealing with short-term lapses will help you to maintain the positive results of your treatment.

AIM

1. Articulate the adherence goal of understanding that making a change takes time and practice—slips can happen. How would you feel if you didn't take your medication one day, either because you forgot or because you were sick and didn't feel like it?

   How would you feel if you didn't follow through with an exercise or diet plan that you had set for yourself? What would you do if that happened?

   _____

   _____

   _____

2. Identify potential barriers. What kinds of thoughts do you think may keep you from restarting your medical regimen if you have a slip?

   _____

   _____

   _____

3. Make a plan and a backup plan:

   Plan: _____

   _____

   Backup plan: _____

   _____

Life-Steps Action Items

1. _____

_____

2. _____

_____

3. _____

_____

4. _____

_____

5. _____

_____

6. _____

_____

7. _____

_____

8. _____

_____

9. _____

_____

10. _____

_____

Review

Review the previous steps with your therapist and write out any action items, such as questions to ask your doctor and reminders to purchase supplies, using the Life-Steps Action Items sheet provided.

Your therapist may schedule a follow-up phone call with you before your next session to review the strategies and reminders you discussed today.

Homework

✎ Begin following the Life-Steps procedures and complete action items before next session

Chapter 4 | *Activity Scheduling*

Goals

▪ To continue monitoring your progress using the CES-D and Weekly Adherence Assessment Form

▪ To create a list of pleasant activities that you can engage in to help improve your mood

▪ To begin monitoring your activities and mood

▪ To identify exercises for home practice

Review of Depression Scale

As you have been doing every week, you should complete the CES-D. Be sure to review your score with your therapist and take note of symptoms that have improved and those that are still problematic. Be sure to record your score on the Progress Summary Chart.

Review of Weekly Adherence Assessment

As you have been doing each week, use the Weekly Adherence Assessment Form to record any medical changes you have experienced since the last session, including changes in your symptoms, emergence of new ones, and any new test results. Rate your adherence and record it on the Progress Summary Chart.

Review of Previous Modules

Each week you should examine your progress in implementing skills from each of the previous modules. It is important to acknowledge

Center for Epidemiologic Studies Depression Scale (CES-D)

Below is a list of the ways you might have felt or behaved. Please tell me how often you have felt this way during the past week.

	During the Past Week			
	Rarely or none of the time (less than 1 day)	**Some or a little of the time (1–2 Days)**	**Occasionally or a moderate amount of time (3–4 days)**	**Most or all of the time (5–7 days)**
1. I was bothered by things that usually don't bother me.	☐	☐	☐	☐
2. I did not feel like eating; my appetite was poor.	☐	☐	☐	☐
3. I felt that I could not shake off the blues even with help from my family or friends.	☐	☐	☐	☐
4. I felt I was just as good as other people.	☐	☐	☐	☐
5. I had trouble keeping my mind on what I was doing.	☐	☐	☐	☐
6. I felt depressed.	☐	☐	☐	☐
7. I felt that everything I did was an effort.	☐	☐	☐	☐
8. I felt hopeful about the future.	☐	☐	☐	☐
9. I thought my life had been a failure.	☐	☐	☐	☐
10. I felt fearful.	☐	☐	☐	☐
11. My sleep was restless.	☐	☐	☐	☐
12. I was happy.	☐	☐	☐	☐
13. I talked less than usual.	☐	☐	☐	☐
14. I felt lonely.	☐	☐	☐	☐
15. People were unfriendly.	☐	☐	☐	☐
16. I enjoyed life.	☐	☐	☐	☐
17. I had crying spells.	☐	☐	☐	☐
18. I felt sad.	☐	☐	☐	☐
19. I felt that people dislike me.	☐	☐	☐	☐
20. I could not get "going."	☐	☐	☐	☐

SCORING: zero for answers in the first column, 1 for answers in the second column, 2 for answers in the third colomn, 3 for answers in the fourth column. The scoring of positive items is reversed. Possible range of scores is zero to 60, with the higher scores indicating the presence of more symptomatology.

Weekly Adherence Assessment Form

You will complete this form at the start of every session. You will work with your therapist to determine your adherence goals during the Life-Steps intervention (module 2) of this treatment program.

Thinking about the **PAST WEEK**, on average how would you rate your ability to adhere to your goal of

_____?

(Check one)

Very poor	Poor	Fair	Good	Very good	Excellent
☐	☐	☐	☐	☐	☐

Thinking about the **PAST WEEK**, on average how would you rate your ability to adhere to your goal of

_____?

(Check one)

Very poor	Poor	Fair	Good	Very good	Excellent
☐	☐	☐	☐	☐	☐

Thinking about the **PAST WEEK**, on average how would you rate your ability to adhere to your goal of

_____?

(Check one)

Very poor	Poor	Fair	Good	Very good	Excellent
☐	☐	☐	☐	☐	☐

Thinking about the **PAST WEEK**, on average how would you rate your ability to adhere to your goal of

_____?

(Check one)

Very poor	Poor	Fair	Good	Very good	Excellent
☐	☐	☐	☐	☐	☐

the successes you have achieved and to problem-solve around any difficulties.

Review: CBT Model of Depression

Review your model of depression, paying close attention to how all of the components interact and contribute to your depression and problems with adhering to your medical routine and taking care of yourself. Remember, the goal of this treatment program is to break the connections between the components and help you overcome your depression.

Review: Life-Steps

The last session focused on teaching you how to effectively follow the medical regimen prescribed by your doctor or other health care provider. Review the importance of self-care behaviors and medical adherence, as well as the AIM problem-solving technique. With the help of your therapist, make additional plans or backup plans for any new strategy that did not work for you over the previous week.

Activity Scheduling

Refer back to your personalized model of depression in chapter 2. Remember that the behavioral component of depression refers to the particular behaviors you do or don't do because you are depressed. If you avoid situations that normally provide you with pleasure and that make you feel competent, your depression may increase or fail to get better. The goal is for you to begin reincorporating pleasant activities into your daily life in an effort to relieve your depression.

We understand that you may not be able to participate in certain activities because of your illness. Your therapist will work with you to brainstorm alternative options. For example, if you are asthmatic and can't engage in physical exercise like hiking or jogging, your therapist may suggest that you begin taking leisurely walks around your neighborhood instead.

Additionally, it will be important, through monitoring, to figure out your limits and pace yourself. For individuals with depression and a chronic illness, it is important to maximize the time when you feel good—to take advantage of this and give yourself the opportunity to do the things you like to do during this time. It is also important to know how to pace yourself. You do not want to get to a point where you do too much and overexert yourself. With monitoring the idea is to get more control and to predict your limits.

Positive Events Checklist

Use the Positive Events Checklist provided to create a list of activities that you used to engage in before you were diagnosed with your illness and became depressed. The goal of this exercise is to identify activities that you can begin to participate in once again that will make you feel more positive and that can be done in conjunction with the limitations of your chronic illness. Try to identify at least a few activities that you can engage in regularly, like walking your dog in the same park every day or joining a book or art club that meets weekly or monthly. The idea is to try to do positive activities every day, even if they seem small.

Activity Log

To help you figure out whether or not reengaging in positive events is helpful, your therapist will ask you to fill out an Activity Log on a daily basis. The purpose of keeping these logs is to help illustrate the association of your mood with the activities you engage in. Sometimes people with depression have "global" views of their daily lives. In fact, there is research to suggest that memories are often mood congruent. This means that if you are feeling depressed, you are more likely to remember negative things that have happened to you in the course of a week than positive things. The idea of the activity log is to help you avoid feeling that an entire week was negative. By looking at your Activity Log you may find that there were some parts of the week that were actually enjoyable. Additionally, the Activity Log can help you figure out what kinds of things are better for you

Table 4.1. Positive Events Checklist

1. Going to lunch with a friend
2. Speaking to a friend on the telephone
3. Going to a movie
4. Relaxing in a park or backyard
5. Reading a book for pleasure
6. Going for a walk with a friend or partner
7. Going out for ice cream or sugar-free frozen yogurt on a warm evening
8. Attending a play or show
9. Playing a game with a child or friend
10. Having a special meal or treat
11. Taking a bubble bath
12. Creating art on your computer
13. Building or upgrading a computer
14. Taking digital photos
15. Baking
16. Creating glass art
17. Organizing pictures
18. Helping other people
19. Volunteering
20. Cooking a gourmet meal
21. Renting a movie
22. Making jewelry
23. Getting a manicure or pedicure
24. Rollerblading
25. Getting involved in your community
26. Donating money to the charity of your choice
27. Joining a gym
28. Playing bocce, racquetball, or squash
29. Snowshoeing
30. Kayaking
31. Redecorating your home
32. Getting a pet (or playing with someone else's dog or cat)
33. Mountain biking
34. Apple picking
35. Weightlifting
36. Playing chess or other board games
37. Going to a comedy club
38. Playing golf / miniature golf
39. Going to the driving range
40. Curling
41. Playing Frisbee
42. Telling jokes and funny stories
43. People watching
44. Going window shopping
45. Stargazing
46. Rock climbing (indoor climbing wall)
47. Blowing bubbles
48. Going to a toy store
49. Bird watching
50. Going on a nature walk
51. Having a cup of tea
52. Playing cards with friends / establishing a "poker night"
53. Going to an arcade
54. Surfing the Internet
55. Downloading songs to your MP3 player
56. Chatting online
57. Watching TV
58. Using TiVo or DVR to record your favorite shows
59. Playing video games online
60. Starting a collection (stamps, coins, shells, etc.)
61. Going on a date
62. Relaxing
63. Jogging, walking, running
64. Thinking I have done a full day's work
65. Listening to music
66. Recalling fond memories
67. Going shopping
68. Lying in the sun
69. Laughing
70. Reading magazines or newspapers
71. Hobbies (model building, scrapbook making, etc.)
72. Spending an evening with good friends
73. Planning a day's activities
74. Meeting new people
75. Eating healthful foods
76. Practicing karate, judo, kickboxing
77. Thinking about retirement
78. Tackling home improvement projects
79. Repairing things around the house
80. Working on car or bicycle or motorcycle
81. Wearing sexy clothes
82. Having quiet evenings
83. Taking care of my plants
84. Buying, selling stock
85. Swimming
86. Doodling, drawing, painting
87. Exercising
88. Going to a party
89. Playing soccer
90. Flying kites
91. Having discussions with friends
92. Having family get-togethers
93. Having safe sex
94. Going camping
95. Singing
96. Arranging flowers
97. Practicing religion (going to church, group praying, etc.)
98. Going to the beach
99. Having class reunions
100. Going skating
101. Going sailboating
102. Planning a trip or vacation
103. Doing something spontaneous
104. Doing needlepoint, crocheting, or knitting
105. Going on a scenic drive
106. Entertaining / having a party

107. Joining a social club (e.g., garden club, Parents without Partners, etc.)
108. Flirting / kissing
109. Playing musical instruments
110. Doing arts and crafts
111. Making a gift for someone
112. Buying music (records, CDs, etc.)
113. Watching sports on television
114. Cooking
115. Going on a hike
116. Writing
117. Buying clothes
118. Going out to dinner
119. Discussing books / joining a book club
120. Sightseeing
121. Gardening
122. Going to a spa
123. Going out for coffee
124. Playing tennis
125. Doing yoga / stretching
126. Being with / playing with children
127. Going to concerts
128. Planning to go to school
129. Refinishing furniture
130. Going bike riding
131. Buying gifts
132. Traveling to national parks
133. Going to a spectator sport (auto racing, horse racing, etc.)
134. Teaching
135. Fishing
136. Playing with animals
137. Acting
138. Writing in a journal
139. Writing and sending letters or e-mails
140. Cleaning
141. Taking an exercise class
142. Watching comedy
143. Taking a class
144. Learning a new language
145. Doing crossword puzzles, word jumbles, playing Sudoku
146. Performing magic tricks
147. Getting a new haircut
148. Going to a stylist
149. Going to a bookstore
150. Buying books
151. Dancing
152. Going on a picnic
153. Meditating
154. Playing volleyball
155. Going to the mountains
156. Splurging / treating yourself
157. Having a political discussion
158. Playing softball
159. Seeing and/or showing photos or slides
160. Playing pool
161. Dressing up and looking nice
162. Reflecting on how I've improved
163. Talking on the phone
164. Going to museums
165. Lighting candles
166. Listening to the radio
167. Getting a massage
168. Saying "I love you"
169. Thinking about my good qualities
170. Taking a sauna or a steam bath
171. Skiing (cross-country or downhill)
172. Whitewater rafting
173. Bowling
174. Woodworking
175. Taking dance classes (ballet, tap, salsa, ballroom, etc.)
176. Sitting in a sidewalk café
177. Having an aquarium
178. Erotica (sex books, movies)
179. Horseback riding
180. Doing something new
181. Doing jigsaw puzzles
182. Thinking I'm a person who can cope
183. Going sledding
184. Going to the mall
185. Making a home video

to be doing and what kinds of things bring you down. Discussion of the pattern of activities and mood is a first step that you and your therapist can take to help you restructure your week and begin to combat depression.

For each day of the week, write down the type of activity you participated in and rate how you felt during it. Use a scale of 1 to 10, where 1 = bad mood and 10 = best mood. Take note of the activities that corresponded to high mood ratings and make an effort to engage in them more frequently.

Activity Log

Rate activities for mood (1–10). 1 = bad mood, 10 = best mood.

	Monday	Tuesday	Wednesday	Thursday	Friday	Saturday	Sunday
Morning							
Afternoon							
Evening							

Activity Log

Rate activities for mood (1–10). 1 = bad mood, 10 = best mood.

	Monday	Tuesday	Wednesday	Thursday	Friday	Saturday	Sunday
Morning	Went to bank–2 Dr. visit–5 Exercised–4	Slept late, stayed in bed, watched TV–2	Bed/TV–2	Read a book–6 Had coffee–4	Watched TV–4	Exercised while listening to music–8 Watched TV–4	Had a nice brunch–5
Afternoon	Took a ride with a friend who is courier all over Eastern Mass–8	Mostly watched TV, hung around the house, used the Internet–2	Hung around the house, used the Internet, watched TV–2	Went out for the afternoon: Visited bookstore–8 Read outside of bookstore–8 Walked around the stores–7	My sister Kathy came by with card for me–8 Talked on phone with a friend–7 Had coffee–5	Went to store–6 Walked to park and read–8	Kathy picked me up and we went to my sister's–8
Evening	Watched TV–4 Took bills to my sister's–4	Watched TV–4	Dinner at my sister's house–8	Cleaned shelves and back hall–6 Watched TV–4	Watched TV–4	Watched TV–4	Dinner party with my sisters for my birthday–8

Figure 4.1.

Example of Completed Activity Log

If you have a physical symptom that is prominent to your illness (for example, fatigue, or a particularly debilitating side effect of a medication), be sure to keep track of that as well. Whenever you participate in an activity, be sure to rate the degree to which you experienced the particular symptom. If you don't experience the symptom, enter 0 for your daily symptom rating. If you are diabetic, you can use the log to record your glucose levels and check the association of this with your mood. Again, this will help you and your therapist keep track of the kinds of things that exacerbate your depression and the kinds of things that make you feel better.

Completing the Activity Log will also help you realize a sense of your limits in terms of your physical symptoms. It is important to monitor symptoms of your illness so you can maximize the frequency and quality of positive activities. Living with a chronic illness may mean that you can't do everything you want to. For example, if you suffer from fatigue, you may want to rest up the day before knowing that you have something to do the next day. This will help ensure that you have the energy for the activity. You may also plan to rest the day after because you will likely be tired.

You may photocopy the Activity Log from the book or download multiple copies from the Treatments *That Work*™ website at http://www.oup.com/us/ttw.

Homework

✎ Continue practicing adherence skills from the Life-Steps module.

✎ Begin incorporating pleasant activities into your daily schedule as per your discussion with your therapist.

✎ Monitor your activity and mood and symptom levels on a daily basis using the Activity Log.

Chapter 5

Adaptive Thinking (Cognitive Restructuring): Part I

Goals

- To continue monitoring your progress using the CES-D and Weekly Adherence Assessment Form

- To introduce you to adaptive thinking (cognitive restructuring)

- To learn about errors in thinking and how to identify your automatic negative thoughts using the Thought Record

- To monitor your automatic thoughts and categorize them according to the list of cognitive distortions

- To identify exercises for home practice

Review of Depression Scale

As you have been doing every week, you should complete the CES-D. Be sure to review your score with your therapist and take note of symptoms that have improved and those that are still problematic. Be sure to record your score on the Progress Summary Chart.

Review of Weekly Adherence Assessment

As you have been doing each week, use the Weekly Adherence Assessment Form to record any medical changes you have experienced since the last session, including changes in your symptoms, emergence of new ones, and any new test results. Rate your adherence and record it on the Progress Summary Chart.

Center for Epidemiologic Studies Depression Scale (CES-D)

Below is a list of the ways you might have felt or behaved. Please tell me how often you have felt this way during the past week.

	During the Past Week			
	Rarely or none of the time (less than 1 day)	Some or a little of the time (1–2 Days)	Occasionally or a moderate amount of time (3–4 days)	Most or all of the time (5–7 days)
1. I was bothered by things that usually don't bother me.	☐	☐	☐	☐
2. I did not feel like eating; my appetite was poor.	☐	☐	☐	☐
3. I felt that I could not shake off the blues even with help from my family or friends.	☐	☐	☐	☐
4. I felt I was just as good as other people.	☐	☐	☐	☐
5. I had trouble keeping my mind on what I was doing.	☐	☐	☐	☐
6. I felt depressed.	☐	☐	☐	☐
7. I felt that everything I did was an effort.	☐	☐	☐	☐
8. I felt hopeful about the future.	☐	☐	☐	☐
9. I thought my life had been a failure.	☐	☐	☐	☐
10. I felt fearful.	☐	☐	☐	☐
11. My sleep was restless.	☐	☐	☐	☐
12. I was happy.	☐	☐	☐	☐
13. I talked less than usual.	☐	☐	☐	☐
14. I felt lonely.	☐	☐	☐	☐
15. People were unfriendly.	☐	☐	☐	☐
16. I enjoyed life.	☐	☐	☐	☐
17. I had crying spells.	☐	☐	☐	☐
18. I felt sad.	☐	☐	☐	☐
19. I felt that people dislike me.	☐	☐	☐	☐
20. I could not get "going."	☐	☐	☐	☐

SCORING: zero for answers in the first column, 1 for answers in the second column, 2 for answers in the third colomn, 3 for answers in the fourth column. The scoring of positive items is reversed. Possible range of scores is zero to 60, with the higher scores indicating the presence of more symptomatology.

Weekly Adherence Assessment Form

You will complete this form at the start of every session. You will work with your therapist to determine your adherence goals during the Life-Steps intervention (module 2) of this treatment program.

Thinking about the **PAST WEEK**, on average how would you rate your ability to adhere to your goal of

_____?

(Check one)

Very poor	Poor	Fair	Good	Very good	Excellent
☐	☐	☐	☐	☐	☐

Thinking about the **PAST WEEK**, on average how would you rate your ability to adhere to your goal of

_____?

(Check one)

Very poor	Poor	Fair	Good	Very good	Excellent
☐	☐	☐	☐	☐	☐

Thinking about the **PAST WEEK**, on average how would you rate your ability to adhere to your goal of

_____?

(Check one)

Very poor	Poor	Fair	Good	Very good	Excellent
☐	☐	☐	☐	☐	☐

Thinking about the **PAST WEEK**, on average how would you rate your ability to adhere to your goal of

_____?

(Check one)

Very poor	Poor	Fair	Good	Very good	Excellent
☐	☐	☐	☐	☐	☐

Review of Previous Modules

Each week you should examine your progress in implementing skills from each of the previous modules. It is important to acknowledge the successes you have achieved and to problem-solve around any difficulties.

Review: CBT Model of Depression

Review your model of depression, paying close attention to how all of the components interact and contribute to your depression and problems with adhering to your medical routine and taking care of yourself. Remember, the goal of this treatment program is to break the connections between the components and help you overcome your depression.

Review: Life-Steps

Review the importance of self-care behaviors and medical adherence, as well as the AIM problem-solving technique. With the help of your therapist, make additional plans or backup plans for any new strategy that did not work for you over the previous week.

Review: Activity Scheduling

In the last session, your therapist introduced you to the Activity Log and instructed you to fill it out on a weekly basis. Review with your therapist your completed log from the previous week, and make note of times when your mood was elevated and times when your mood was depressed. What sorts of activities made you feel good and more positive? Try to engage in these activities more often.

Adaptive Thinking/Cognitive Restructuring

People with depression tend to engage in negative thinking. Having a medical illness to manage can make this even worse. Adaptive thinking, or cognitive restructuring, is a method of systematically teaching yourself how to figure out whether you are doing this and whether there are more adaptive, better ways to think about things. Refer back to the model of your depression in chapter 2 and the thoughts you listed. Remember, the cognitive component of depression consists of the negative thoughts that people have when they are depressed.

It is important to note that this technique of thinking more adaptively (called cognitive restructuring) is different from "positive thinking." Positive thinking means to randomly replace negative thoughts with positive thoughts. This is not an effective way of dealing with negative thoughts and is not the goal of this exercise. The goal of cognitive restructuring is to come up with alternative thoughts that are true and realistic and that make you feel better. For example, this technique will help you deal with the true realities of coping with a chronic illness but will also help you try to cope with it in a way that is realistic and most helpful for your situation.

Cognitive Distortions List

Your therapist will introduce you to cognitive restructuring by first having you review a list of cognitive distortions or errors in thinking. Cognitive distortions maintain negative thinking and help to maintain negative emotions. Negative and inaccurate thoughts and beliefs can lead to poor behavioral consequences, including avoidance, feelings of helplessness and hopelessness, depression, the inability to take good care of yourself, and poor adherence to medications.

Review the cognitive distortions list with your therapist and identify the types of thoughts that apply to you the most. Give specific examples of times when you think you have had the various types of thoughts listed.

All-or-nothing thinking: You see things in black-and-white categories. For example, you have to change your *entire life* because you are taking medicines for your illness, or *all* aspects of a project need to be completed immediately, or if your performance falls short of perfect, you see it as a total failure. For example, you are trying to eat a healthy diet, but one day you "slip up" and overeat something you know is not healthy. The next day, you say to yourself, "Either I stick to my diet or it's no use! Since I messed up yesterday, it doesn't matter what I eat today, the rest of the weekend, or the rest of the month."

Overgeneralization: You see a single negative event as a never-ending pattern. You have a low blood sugar count (or maybe a really high one) after you've been trying to make some changes to your diet and exercise, and you say to yourself, "I'm never going to be able to get my diabetes in control! What I do makes no difference and I'm just no good at taking care of myself. Nothing will ever change anyway!"

Mental filter: You pick out a single negative detail and dwell on it exclusively, so that your vision of all reality becomes darkened, like the drop of ink that discolors the entire beaker of water. For example, you are working on increasing your glucose monitoring and physical activity and trying to eat a better daily diet. Although this has been going well and you've made consistent improvements, you only focus on the negatives. For example, you might think, "Well, yeah, I've been trying but it's not going to make any difference because I haven't lost weight yet." You focus on negative information and ignore all the positives.

Disqualifying the positive: You reject positive experiences or successes by insisting they "don't count" for one reason or another. In this way, you can maintain a negative belief that is contradicted by your everyday experiences. For example, maybe you say to yourself, "They are just being nice" when someone gives you a compliment. For instance, if someone compliments your clothes, you say, "Oh, this old thing?" This is a destructive negative thought because what you are telling yourself is that you are second-rate and not worth the compliment. Instead, you can choose to accept the positive and when someone compliments you, say "thank you!" You might even think, "how nice of them to notice," because you have already focused on your positive qualities.

Jumping to conclusions: You make a negative interpretation even though there are no facts that convincingly support your conclusion.

Mind reading: You arbitrarily conclude that someone is reacting negatively to you, and you don't bother to check this out. For example, you assume that the person you are attracted to knows you are HIV-infected and therefore will not want to date you.

Fortune-telling: You anticipate that things will turn out badly, and you feel that your prediction is a predetermined fact. For example, you predict that no matter what you do, you will never lose the weight you need to in order to stay healthy.

Magnification/minimization: You exaggerate the importance of things (such as the degree to which your illness affects a situation, your life, or other people; your mistakes; or someone else's achievement) or you inappropriately shrink things until they appear tiny (your own desirable qualities, your ability to do something despite having a chronic illness, or the other's imperfections).

Catastrophizing: You attribute extreme and horrible consequences to the outcomes of events. For example, you might interpret one slip with medications or monitoring as meaning that you will never be able to manage your regimen. One mistake at work = being fired from your job; one bad day = you will be unhappy forever.

Emotional reasoning: You assume that your negative emotions necessarily reflect the way things really are: "I feel it, so it must be true." "I feel bad about myself for being overweight and therefore other people will think I am a bad person." Another example might be, "I feel guilty, so I deserve this" or "I feel depressed, so I must be a loser."

"Should" statements: You try to motivate yourself with "shoulds" and "shouldn'ts," as if you need to be punished before you could be expected to do anything. When you direct "should" statements toward others, you feel anger, frustration, and resentment. For example, you believe that you "should" clean the house every day, but you do not have the time to do it, and then you feel guilty.

Labeling and mislabeling: This is an extreme form of overgeneralization. Instead of describing an error, you attach a negative label to yourself or others. For example, you may forget to take your medications and say to yourself, "I'm stupid" or "I'm no good at this."

Personalization: You see negative events as indicative of some negative characteristic of yourself or others, or you take responsibility for events that were not your doing. Your significant other might come home in a bad mood after work, and you might say to yourself, "she/he is mad at me," or "she/he doesn't even care about me anymore."

Maladaptive thinking: You focus on a thought that may be true but over which you have no control (e.g., "my abilities are more limited than they were before I was sick"). Excessively thinking about it can be self-critical or can distract you from an important task or from attempting new behaviors.

Automatic Thoughts

Automatic thoughts are thoughts that automatically come to mind when a particular situation occurs. We all have automatic thoughts. There is a constant stream of comments, interpretations, and judgments that run through our heads as we observe things around us and respond to situations on a daily basis. For example, when running late for work, you might say to yourself, "Damn it! I'm late because I was so tired this morning. I should have gone to bed earlier last night." Instead of reacting to the reality of a situation, individuals with depression tend to react more negatively than the situation would warrant. Sometimes this involves negative predictions of what will happen. Sometimes it involves interpreting the situation in a way that is consistent with a negative view of yourself. When you are depressed, your automatic thoughts are more likely to be negative in nature. Again, your thoughts tend to be consistent with your mood. So, if you are depressed, it is more likely that you will be thinking negatively, and you may not even realize it. Going back to our example of running late for work, when depressed you might tend to be more extreme and self-blaming in your automatic thoughts. You might say, "Damn it! I'm running late for work and now I'm going to look bad in front of everyone. I can never get it together in the morning to leave the house on time. If I can't do that, what can I do? I don't even feel like going in to face everyone."

Sometimes it is difficult to understand the concept of automatic thoughts. Here is an illustration. Think about when you first learned to drive a car. At the age of 15 or 16, trying to coordinate many tasks at once, you had to be specifically conscious of handling the steering wheel, remembering to signal for turns, staying exactly in your lane, averting other traffic, trying to park, and doing many tasks at the same time that required your total attention.

Now, think about driving today. You probably know how to drive without thinking actively about what you are doing. The process of driving has become automatic. You probably don't even remember thinking about all of these steps because they have become automatic.

In the same way that driving has become automatic, so can your interpretations of various situations, which can result in a continuation of depressed mood. When people are depressed for an extended period of time, they continue to interpret neutral or even positive situations in ways that are consistent with their negative view of themselves, the future, and the past. For example, we had a client with diabetes who was overweight and had depression. She maintained the belief that she was ugly and that therefore no one would want to talk with her or be her friend. When she would go to events she would not approach new people or talk to them. When people would approach her, she would shy away from maintaining a conversation because of this negative view of herself. This pattern of thinking and behavior became automatic—and reinforced itself—because, in the end, it became a self-fulfilling prophecy. People did not speak to her because she avoided them due to her thoughts and beliefs about herself.

Identifying Automatic Thoughts

The Thought Record is a tool that was developed to help you learn how to identify, slow down, and restructure negative automatic thoughts. Pick a situation or time from your most recent Activity Log when you noted that your mood was especially low. With your therapist's help, come up with the automatic thoughts you had during that time and list them on the Thought Record on page 76.

In column 1 of the Thought Record, write a brief description of the problem. When did it take place, where were you, who were you with, what was going on? In this column you need to be as objective as possible. Describe the situation in just one or two sentences but as if you were observing it. Column 2 is for recording your thoughts. What was going through your mind at the time? What were you saying to yourself about the situation, other people, and your role in the situation? In this column, it is important to use a small number of

Thought Record

Time and situation	Automatic thoughts (what was going through your head?)	Mood and intensity of mood (0–100)	Cognitive distortions (match thoughts from list)	Rational response

Thought Record

Time and situation	Automatic thoughts (what was going through your head?)	Mood and intensity of mood (0–100)	Cognitive distortions (match thoughts from list)	Rational response
Tues. afternoon: Went to cookout with my girlfriend and daughter.	Good memories (at first) of wife who passed away.	First, felt really good (80)		
	I don't take care of myself well enough.	A little sad (60)	"Should" thinking Fortune-telling	
	Because of this, I won't live long enough to have these kinds of outings to enjoy with my family.	Very sad and guilty (95)	"Should" thinking Labeling	
	My daughter lost her mother and has a horrible father.			
Weds. morning: I woke up and knew it was time to take my medications but I had to push myself to get out of bed and so I just didn't take them.	I'm never going to be healthy.	Disappointed in myself (80)	Catastrophizing	
	I can't take care of myself.	Hopeless (95)	Labeling	
	I am a horrible person.			

Figure 5.1

Example of Completed Thought Record Up to Cognitive Distortions Column short sentences to describe each thought. To be most effective, you need to list each thought you have individually. This is different from journaling or keeping a diary in which you record all thoughts and feelings in a stream-of-consciousness sort of way. Many people find it difficult to use discrete sentences and to list their thoughts individually. However, as with all skills, the more you practice the easier it becomes.

Column 3 is for recording your mood and the emotions you experienced. Rate the intensity of each feeling on a scale of 0–100, where 0 = lowest intensity and 100 = most intense.

Column 4 is for matching your thoughts to any of the thinking errors from the list of cognitive distortions. Some of your thoughts may correspond to more than one cognitive distortion. Work with your therapist to determine the most common types of distortions you experience. Discuss each one and highlight the connection between thinking and mood.

Column 5 should be left blank for now. You will learn about rational responses in the next chapter.

You may photocopy the Thought Record from this book or download multiple copies from the Treatments *ThatWork*™ website at http://www.oup.com/us/ttw. We have also provided a sample, filled-out Thought Record in figure 5.1 for you to use as a model when completing your own.

Homework

✎ Continue using and reviewing skills from previous modules and sessions.

✎ Read the Preliminary Instructions for Cognitive Restructuring provided at the end of this chapter.

✎ Use the Thought Record to identify automatic thoughts and match them to cognitive distortions for at least two situations that you also listed on the Activity Log during the week.

✎ Be sure to use only the first four columns of the Thought Record, as rational responses have yet to be discussed.

The purpose of Thought Records is to identify automatic thoughts in situations that lead to depression.

The first step in learning to think in more useful ways is to become more aware of these thoughts and their relationship to your mood. If you are anticipating a stressful situation or a task that is making you feel overwhelmed, write out your thoughts regarding this situation. If a situation has already passed and you find that you are thinking about it negatively, list your thoughts for this situation. You should also record your thoughts throughout the week when you are feeling sad or depressed.

To start with, use the **first four** columns of the Thought Record provided.

The **first column** is a description of the situation.

The **second column** is for you to list your thoughts during a stressful, overwhelming, or uncontrollable situation.

The **third column** is for you to write down what emotions you are having and what your mood is like when thinking these thoughts (e.g., depressed, sad, angry).

The **fourth column** is for you to see whether your thoughts match the list of "cognitive distortions." These may include:

- All-or-nothing thinking
- Overgeneralizations
- Jumping to conclusions: Fortune-telling/mind reading
- Magnification/minimization
- Emotional reasoning
- "Should" statements
- Labeling and mislabeling
- Personalization
- Maladaptive thinking

Chapter 6

Adaptive Thinking (Cognitive Restructuring): Part II

Goals

- To continue monitoring your progress using the CES-D and Weekly Adherence Assessment Form

- To discuss rational responses and how to form them

- To identify exercises for home practice

Review of Depression Scale

As you have been doing every week, you should complete the CES-D. Be sure to review your score with your therapist and take note of symptoms that have improved and those that are still problematic. Be sure to record your score on the Progress Summary Chart.

Review of Weekly Adherence Assessment

As you have been doing each week, use the Weekly Adherence Assessment Form to record any medical changes you have experienced since the last session, including changes in your symptoms, emergence of new ones, and any new test results. Rate your adherence and record it on the Progress Summary Chart.

Review of Previous Material

Each week you should examine your progress in implementing skills from each of the previous modules. It is important to acknowledge the successes you have achieved and to problem-solve around any difficulties.

Center for Epidemiologic Studies Depression Scale (CES-D)

Below is a list of the ways you might have felt or behaved. Please tell me how often you have felt this way during the past week.

	During the Past Week			
	Rarely or none of the time (less than 1 day)	Some or a little of the time (1–2 Days)	Occasionally or a moderate amount of time (3–4 days)	Most or all of the time (5–7 days)
1. I was bothered by things that usually don't bother me.	☐	☐	☐	☐
2. I did not feel like eating; my appetite was poor.	☐	☐	☐	☐
3. I felt that I could not shake off the blues even with help from my family or friends.	☐	☐	☐	☐
4. I felt I was just as good as other people.	☐	☐	☐	☐
5. I had trouble keeping my mind on what I was doing.	☐	☐	☐	☐
6. I felt depressed.	☐	☐	☐	☐
7. I felt that everything I did was an effort.	☐	☐	☐	☐
8. I felt hopeful about the future.	☐	☐	☐	☐
9. I thought my life had been a failure.	☐	☐	☐	☐
10. I felt fearful.	☐	☐	☐	☐
11. My sleep was restless.	☐	☐	☐	☐
12. I was happy.	☐	☐	☐	☐
13. I talked less than usual.	☐	☐	☐	☐
14. I felt lonely.	☐	☐	☐	☐
15. People were unfriendly.	☐	☐	☐	☐
16. I enjoyed life.	☐	☐	☐	☐
17. I had crying spells.	☐	☐	☐	☐
18. I felt sad.	☐	☐	☐	☐
19. I felt that people dislike me.	☐	☐	☐	☐
20. I could not get "going."	☐	☐	☐	☐

SCORING: zero for answers in the first column, 1 for answers in the second column, 2 for answers in the third colomn, 3 for answers in the fourth column. The scoring of positive items is reversed. Possible range of scores is zero to 60, with the higher scores indicating the presence of more symptomatology.

Weekly Adherence Assessment Form

You will complete this form at the start of every session. You will work with your therapist to determine your adherence goals during the Life-Steps intervention (module 2) of this treatment program.

Thinking about the **PAST WEEK**, on average how would you rate your ability to adhere to your goal of

_____?

(Check one)

Very poor	Poor	Fair	Good	Very good	Excellent
☐	☐	☐	☐	☐	☐

Thinking about the **PAST WEEK**, on average how would you rate your ability to adhere to your goal of

_____?

(Check one)

Very poor	Poor	Fair	Good	Very good	Excellent
☐	☐	☐	☐	☐	☐

Thinking about the **PAST WEEK**, on average how would you rate your ability to adhere to your goal of

_____?

(Check one)

Very poor	Poor	Fair	Good	Very good	Excellent
☐	☐	☐	☐	☐	☐

Thinking about the **PAST WEEK**, on average how would you rate your ability to adhere to your goal of

_____?

(Check one)

Very poor	Poor	Fair	Good	Very good	Excellent
☐	☐	☐	☐	☐	☐

Review: CBT Model of Depression

Review your model of depression, paying close attention to how all of the components interact and contribute to your depression and problems with adhering to your medical routine and taking care of yourself. Remember, the goal of this treatment program is to break the connections between the components and help you overcome your depression.

Review: Life-Steps

Review the importance of self-care behaviors and medical adherence, as well as the AIM problem-solving technique. With the help of your therapist, make additional plans or backup plans for any new strategy that did not work for you over the previous week.

Review: Activity Scheduling

Review your completed Activity Log from the previous week with your therapist and make note of times when your mood was elevated and times when your mood was depressed. What sorts of activities made you feel good and more positive? Try to engage in these activities more often.

Review: Cognitive Restructuring: Part I

Review your completed Thought Records from the previous week with your therapist. If you were not able to complete any Thought Records, try to identify the obstacles that may have interfered, and use the problem-solving skills to determine the best way to work on automatic thinking.

If you didn't complete any records, it may be useful to do so in session with your therapist.

Review each situation and the automatic thoughts and thinking errors you identified. Did you see any patterns?

Rational Responses

In this session you will learn strategies for correcting thinking errors and developing more helpful thoughts. Our goal is to help you transform the unhelpful, interfering thoughts into more supportive, coaching thoughts. In order to understand how powerful your thoughts can be, we like to tell a coaching story.

Coaching Story

This is a story about Little League baseball. I talk about Little League baseball because of the amazing parents and coaches involved. And by "amazing" I don't mean good. I mean extreme.

But this story doesn't start with the coaches or the parents. It starts with Johnny, who is a Little League player in the outfield. His job is to catch fly balls and return them to the infield players. On this particular day of our story, Johnny is in the outfield. And "crack!"—one of the players on the other team hits a fly ball. The ball is coming to Johnny. Johnny raises his glove. The ball is coming to him, it is coming to him . . . and it goes over his head. Johnny misses the ball, and the other team scores a run.

Now there are a number of ways a coach can respond to this situation. Let's take Coach A first. Coach A is the type of coach who will come out on the field and shout:

> *I can't believe you missed that ball! Anyone could have caught it! My dog could have caught it! You screw up like that again and you'll be sitting on the bench! That was lousy!*

Coach A then storms off the field. At this point, if Johnny is anything like I am, he is standing there, tense, tight, trying not to cry, and praying that another ball is not hit to him. If a ball does come to him, Johnny will probably miss it. After all, he is tense, tight, and may see four balls coming to him because of the tears in his eyes. Also, if we are Johnny's parents, we may see more profound changes after the game: Johnny, who typically places his baseball glove on the mantle, now throws it under his bed. And before the next game, he may complain that his stomach hurts, that perhaps he should not go to the game. This is the scenario with Coach A.

Now let's go back to the original event and play it differently. Johnny has just missed the fly ball, and now Coach B comes out on the field. Coach B says:

> *Well, you missed that one. Here is what I want you to remember: fly balls always look like they are farther away than they really are. Also, it is much easier to run forward than to back up. Because of this, I want you to prepare for the ball by taking a few extra steps backward. Run forward if you need to, but try to catch it at chest level, so you can adjust your hand if you misjudge the ball. Let's see how you do next time.*

Coach B leaves the field. How does Johnny feel? Well, he is not happy. After all, he missed the ball—but there are a number of important differences from the way he felt with Coach A. He is not as tense or tight, and if a fly ball does come to him, he knows what to do differently to catch it. And because he does not have tears in his eyes, he may actually see the ball accurately. He may catch the next one.

So, if we were the type of parent who eventually wants Johnny to make the major leagues, we would pick Coach B, because he teaches Johnny how to be a more effective player. Johnny knows what to do differently, may catch more balls, and may excel at the game. But if we don't care whether Johnny makes the major leagues—because baseball is a game and one is supposed to be able to enjoy a game—then we would still pick Coach B. We pick Coach B because we care whether Johnny enjoys the game. With Coach B, Johnny knows what to do differently; he is not tight, tense, and ready to cry; he may catch a few balls; and he may enjoy the game. And he may continue to place his glove on the mantel.

Now, while we may all select Coach B for Johnny, we rarely choose the view of Coach B for the way we talk to ourselves. Think about your last mistake. Did you say, "I can't believe I did that! I am so stupid! What a jerk!" These are Coach A thoughts, and they have approximately the same effect on us that they do on Johnny. They make us feel tense and tight, and sometimes make us feel like crying. And this style of coaching rarely makes us do better in the future. If you are only concerned about productivity (making the major leagues), you would pick Coach B. And if you were concerned with enjoying life, while guiding yourself effectively for both joy and productivity, you would still pick Coach B.

Keep in mind that we are not talking about how we coach ourselves in a baseball game. We are talking about how we coach ourselves in life, and our enjoyment of life.

During the next week, I would like you to listen to see how you are coaching yourself. And if you hear Coach A, remember this story and see if you can replace Coach A with Coach B.

This story is meant to help you recognize negative, unhelpful thoughts as they pop up (Coach A thoughts) and learn to develop more supportive, rational thinking (Coach B thoughts). It's also meant to illustrate that many times, negative thinking (Coach A) not only makes us feel worse but also often has a negative influence on our behavior. Coach A didn't tell Johnny anything that would help him catch the ball next time; he just made him feel terrible. In fact, because he made Johnny feel so awful about himself, he might have made it more likely that Johnny will not want to practice as much anymore or maybe even give up on baseball altogether. Just as it's important to see the behavioral consequences of Coach A's statements for Johnny, it's important for us to see the behavioral consequences of our own negative thoughts for our own lives. It's important to ask yourself, "What's the consequence of thinking this way?" or "What is choosing to think this way going to do for me?"

Let's go back to one of your completed Thought Records from last week. Review the automatic thoughts and thinking errors that you identified. If you have not completed a Thought Record yet, you should begin a new one now—looking at a situation or time from the previous week when you felt down. First, as before, be sure you have a good list of automatic thoughts and match them with cognitive distortions. The next step is to evaluate the helpfulness of each thought. To help you objectively evaluate these thoughts, ask yourself the following questions.

- Can I look at this in a way that is still true, but more helpful to me and to the situation?

- What are the consequences of thinking this way?

- What is the evidence that this thought is true?

- Is there an alternate explanation?

- What is the worst thing that can happen? Has this situation unreasonably grown in importance?

- What would a good coach say about this situation?

- Have I done what I can do to control it? If I were to do anything else, would this help or hinder the situation?

- Am I worrying excessively about this?

- What would a good friend say to me about this situation? What would I say to a good friend about this situation if he or she were going through it?

- Why is this statement a cognitive distortion?

The fifth column of the Thought Record is for recording rational responses. The rational response is a statement that you can say to yourself to try to feel better about the situation. Keep in mind that we are not asking you to overlook all negative aspects of your thoughts. The idea is to come up with a more balanced, objective, and helpful way of thinking about the situation.

See figure 6.1 for a sample Thought Record with rational responses that you can use as a model when filling out your own.

The goal here is for you to learn this skill of adaptive thinking so that you can apply it on your own. We find that it is helpful for most people to start by using the form and writing the thoughts down, because it helps identify the thoughts systematically and then "talk back" to negative automatic thinking that contributes to your depression. Writing it out can help you more objectively evaluate the situation and think more clearly. It can help remove the distorted lens of depression from your negative interpretation of the situation. Ideally, after practicing by using this form, your thinking will begin to change, so that this new way of thinking becomes more automatic and/or you slowly start doing the steps outlined in your head.

Homework

✎ Continue using and reviewing skills from previous modules and sessions.

✎ Use your Thought Record to list automatic thoughts, thinking errors, and rational responses for situations for the coming week.

✎ Complete Thought Records for at least two situations during the week.

✎ Read the Developing a Rational Response handout provided at the end of this chapter.

Thought Record

Time and situation	Automatic thoughts (what was going through your head?)	Mood and intensity of mood (0–100)	Cognitive distortions (match thoughts from list)	Rational response
Tues. afternoon: Went to cookout with my girlfriend and daughter.	Good memories (at first) of wife who passed away.	First, felt really good (80)		I can only do my best in terms of taking care of myself.
	I don't take care of myself well enough.	A little sad (60)	"Should" thinking Fortune-telling	Although I have an illness, there are things I can do to take good care of myself and can therefore live a longer life.
	Because of this, I won't live long enough to have these kinds of outings to enjoy with my family.	Very sad and guilty (95)	"Should" thinking Labeling	I do the best I can to take care of my daughter.
	My daughter lost her mother and has a horrible father.			
Weds. morning: I woke up and knew it was time to take my medications but I had to push myself to get out of bed and so I just didn't take them.	I'm never going to be healthy.	Disappointed in myself (80)	Catastrophizing Labeling	I have been better at taking my meds. Today was a slip.
	I can't take care of myself.	Hopeless (95)		Missing meds one morning does not mean I am a horrible person.
	I am a horrible person.			

Figure 6.1

Example of Completed Thought Record

Thought Record

Time and situation	Automatic thoughts (what was going through your head?)	Mood and intensity of mood (0–100)	Cognitive distortions (match thoughts from list)	Rational response

Adaptive Thinking: Developing a Rational Response

The purpose of cognitive restructuring is to help promote adaptive and balanced thinking when you are depressed.

Throughout the week when you are feeling sad or overwhelmed, continue to use the Thought Record to list your thoughts for each situation on your Activity Log when you noted that your mood was low. If you are anticipating a stressful situation or a task that is making you feel overwhelmed, write out your thoughts regarding this situation. If a situation has already passed and you find that you are thinking about it negatively, list your thoughts for this situation. Becoming aware of and changing negative thoughts will be a process. At first, you may only be able to recognize distortions in your thinking in hindsight, after the emotions of the moment have "cooled down." That's a great first step, and it's important not to be critical of yourself for not having been aware of the distortion in the moment. Over time, you may recognize your negative thoughts more quickly, and, eventually, you will be able to replace them with more adaptive thoughts that can themselves become automatic.

The **first column** is a description of the situation.

The **second column** is for you to list your thoughts during a stressful, overwhelming, or uncontrollable situation.

The **third column** is for you to write down what emotions you are having and what your mood is like when thinking these thoughts (e.g., depressed, sad, angry).

The **fourth column** is for you to see whether your thoughts match the list of "cognitive distortions" These may include:

All-or-nothing thinking	Emotional reasoning
Overgeneralizations	"Should" statements
Jumping to conclusions: Fortune-telling/ mind reading	Labeling and mislabeling
	Personalization
Magnification/minimization	Maladaptive thinking

In the **last column**, try to come up with a rational response to each thought, or to the most important negative thought. The rational response is a statement that you can say to yourself to try to feel better about the situation. Questions to help come up with this rational response can include:

What is the evidence that this thought is true?

Is there an alternate explanation?

What is the worst thing that can happen?

Has this situation unreasonably grown in importance?

What would a good coach say about this situation?

Have I done what I can do to control it?

If I were to do anything else, would this help or hinder the situation?

Am I worrying excessively about this?

What would a good friend say to me about this situation?

What would I say to a good friend about this situation if he or she were going through it?

Why is this statement a cognitive distortion?

What are the consequences of thinking this way?

Chapter 7   *Problem Solving*

Goals

- To continue monitoring your progress using the CES-D and Weekly Adherence Assessment Form

- To learn how to use problem solving to overcome difficulties with completing tasks or finding solutions

- To identify exercises for home practice

Review of Depression Scale

As you have been doing every week, you should complete the CES-D. Be sure to review your score with your therapist and take note of symptoms that have improved and those that are still problematic. Be sure to record your score on the Progress Summary Chart.

Review of Weekly Adherence Assessment

As you have been doing each week, use the Weekly Adherence Assessment Form to record any medical changes you have experienced since the last session, including changes in your symptoms, emergence of new ones, and any new test results. Rate your adherence and record it on the Progress Summary Chart.

Review of Previous Modules

Each week you should examine your progress in implementing skills from each of the previous modules. It is important to acknowledge the successes you have achieved and to problem-solve around any difficulties.

Center for Epidemiologic Studies Depression Scale (CES-D)

Below is a list of the ways you might have felt or behaved. Please tell me how often you have felt this way during the past week.

	During the Past Week			
	Rarely or none of the time (less than 1 day)	Some or a little of the time (1–2 Days)	Occasionally or a moderate amount of time (3–4 days)	Most or all of the time (5–7 days)
1. I was bothered by things that usually don't bother me.	☐	☐	☐	☐
2. I did not feel like eating; my appetite was poor.	☐	☐	☐	☐
3. I felt that I could not shake off the blues even with help from my family or friends.	☐	☐	☐	☐
4. I felt I was just as good as other people.	☐	☐	☐	☐
5. I had trouble keeping my mind on what I was doing.	☐	☐	☐	☐
6. I felt depressed.	☐	☐	☐	☐
7. I felt that everything I did was an effort.	☐	☐	☐	☐
8. I felt hopeful about the future.	☐	☐	☐	☐
9. I thought my life had been a failure.	☐	☐	☐	☐
10. I felt fearful.	☐	☐	☐	☐
11. My sleep was restless.	☐	☐	☐	☐
12. I was happy.	☐	☐	☐	☐
13. I talked less than usual.	☐	☐	☐	☐
14. I felt lonely.	☐	☐	☐	☐
15. People were unfriendly.	☐	☐	☐	☐
16. I enjoyed life.	☐	☐	☐	☐
17. I had crying spells.	☐	☐	☐	☐
18. I felt sad.	☐	☐	☐	☐
19. I felt that people dislike me.	☐	☐	☐	☐
20. I could not get "going."	☐	☐	☐	☐

SCORING: zero for answers in the first column, 1 for answers in the second column, 2 for answers in the third colomn, 3 for answers in the fourth column. The scoring of positive items is reversed. Possible range of scores is zero to 60, with the higher scores indicating the presence of more symptomatology.

Weekly Adherence Assessment Form

You will complete this form at the start of every session. You will work with your therapist to determine your adherence goals during the Life-Steps intervention (module 2) of this treatment program.

Thinking about the **PAST WEEK**, on average how would you rate your ability to adhere to your goal of

_____?

(Check one)

Very poor	Poor	Fair	Good	Very good	Excellent
☐	☐	☐	☐	☐	☐

Thinking about the **PAST WEEK**, on average how would you rate your ability to adhere to your goal of

_____?

(Check one)

Very poor	Poor	Fair	Good	Very good	Excellent
☐	☐	☐	☐	☐	☐

Thinking about the **PAST WEEK**, on average how would you rate your ability to adhere to your goal of

_____?

(Check one)

Very poor	Poor	Fair	Good	Very good	Excellent
☐	☐	☐	☐	☐	☐

Thinking about the **PAST WEEK**, on average how would you rate your ability to adhere to your goal of

_____?

(Check one)

Very poor	Poor	Fair	Good	Very good	Excellent
☐	☐	☐	☐	☐	☐

Review: CBT Model of Depression

Review your model of depression, paying close attention to how all of the components interact and contribute to your depression and problems with adhering to your medical routine and taking care of yourself. Remember, the goal of this treatment program is to break the connections between the components and help you overcome your depression.

Review: Life-Steps

Review the importance of self-care behaviors and medical adherence, as well as the AIM problem-solving technique. With the help of your therapist, make additional plans or backup plans for any new strategy that did not work for you over the previous week.

Review: Activity Scheduling

Review your completed Activity Log from the previous week with your therapist and make note of times when your mood was elevated and times when your mood was depressed. What sorts of activities made you feel good and more positive? Try to engage in these activities more often.

Review: Adaptive Thinking: Parts I and II

Review your Thought Records from the previous week and discuss with your therapist any difficulties you may be having with identifying, labeling, and challenging your automatic negative thoughts. If necessary, complete a Thought Record in session to review cognitive restructuring skills.

Problem-Solving Strategies

In this section, we focus on learning to recognize when you are having difficulty completing a task or are becoming overwhelmed and cannot figure out exactly where to start. The reason we call problems "problems" is that there is no easy solution at hand; usually any solution has serious pros and cons. This can sometimes lead to procrastination or avoidance of doing something about the problem. Procrastinating or avoiding the issue does nothing to solve the problem. In fact, avoidance can sometimes make the problem worse in the long run. We have found that for people with depression, it becomes harder than usual to solve life's problems. Additionally, coping with a chronic medical illness usually comes with a new set of challenges that can require proactive problem solving. Systematic techniques to help problem-solve these challenges can be important.

Once you recognize that there is a problem, you can use these problem-solving strategies to help. Your therapist will introduce to you the two skills necessary for effective problem solving. They are:

1. Selecting a plan of action

2. Breaking down an overwhelming task into manageable steps

Developing an action plan can be helpful when it is difficult to determine how to resolve a problem, or when the number of possible solutions becomes overwhelming, or when you think that there are no solutions. Selecting an action plan involves the five steps in problem-solving listed here.

The Five Steps of Problem-Solving

Use these instructions in conjunction with the Problem-Solving Sheet provided on page 99.

Step 1. Articulate the Problem

Try to describe the problem in as few words as possible using one or two sentences at the most. Examples include:

- I cannot decide whether I should switch my health care provider.

- I cannot decide what to do about my housing situation.

- I am in debt due to medical expenses.

Step 2. List All Possible Solutions

In the first column of the Problem-Solving Sheet, write down a number of solutions for your problem, regardless of how possible they are, what the consequences may be, or whether or not they are silly or outrageous. The idea is to generate a list of as many solutions as possible. Really try to brainstorm here as much as possible. Remember, one solution is to just continue doing what you've been doing all along (e.g., avoiding it, procrastinating, etc).

Step 3. List the Pros and Cons of Each Solution

Now is the time to go through and systematically and as realistically as possible appraise each solution. In the Pros and Cons columns of the sheet, figure out what you really think would happen if you selected that solution. List the pros (advantages) and cons (disadvantages) of each.

Step 4. Rate Each Solution

Using the final column of the sheet, rate the pros and cons of each solution on a scale from 1 to 10. Try to be as objective as possible, but include the relative difficulty of applying the solution. For example, if the problem is that you are too tired (because of your illness) to maintain your current work schedule, one solution might be to speak with your boss about it. When making the rating, you should factor in whether this will be anxiety-provoking or embarrassing, as well as whether it will be likely to have the desired outcome.

Step 5. Implement the Best Solution

Now that you have rated each option on a scale of 1 to 10, review each rating. Look at the solution that is rated the highest. Determine whether this is really the solution that you would like to pick. If so, use the other skills (for example, adaptive thinking) you have learned in this treatment program to implement it.

You may photocopy the Problem-Solving Sheet from the book or download multiple copies from the Treatments *That Work*™ website at http://www.oup.com/us/ttw.

Problem-Solving Sheet

Statement of the problem: _____

Instructions:

1) List all of the possible solutions that you can think of. List them even if you think they don't make sense, or you don't think you would do them. The point is to come up with *as many solutions as possible.*
2) List the pros and cons of each solution.
3) After listing the pros and cons of each, review the whole list, and give a rating to each solution.
4) Use additional copies of this sheet as needed (even if it's for the same problem).

Possible Solution	Pros of Solution	Cons of Solution	Overall Rating of Solution (1–10)

Breaking Large Tasks Down Into Manageable Steps

The next part of problem solving involves trying to break the solution down into manageable steps. If a task seems overwhelming, we are much more likely to procrastinate and not even attempt to start working on it. Even if the solution is clear, it may just feel easier to put off working on the overwhelming task. By learning how to break large tasks down into smaller, more manageable steps, you will increase the likelihood that you will *start* (and therefore eventually complete) important tasks.

Steps for Breaking Large Tasks Into Manageable Steps

1. Choose a problem that exists for you that you are avoiding.

2. List the steps that must be completed. This can be done using small note cards or plain paper. Ask questions such as, "What is the first thing that I would need to do to make this happen? What is next?"

3. For each step, make sure that it is manageable. Ask yourself, "Is this something that I could realistically complete in one day?" and "Is this something that I would want to put off doing?"

Once you have the step written down, look at it and ask yourself, Is this too much? If the step itself is overwhelming, then break that step down into further steps. Don't be afraid to have more steps.

Homework

✎ Continue using and reviewing skills from previous modules and sessions.

✎ Use the formal problem-solving method when necessary and record possible solutions on the Problem-Solving Sheet.

Chapter 8

Relaxation Training and Diaphragmatic Breathing

Goals

- To continue monitoring your progress using the CES-D and Weekly Adherence Assessment Form

- To learn diaphragmatic breathing and progressive muscle relaxation (PMR)

- To record your breathing exercise and relaxation training on the Breathing Retraining and Progressive Muscle Relaxation Practice Log

- To identify exercises for home practice

Review of Depression Scale

As you have been doing every week, you should complete the CES-D. Be sure to review your score with your therapist and take note of symptoms that have improved and those that are still problematic. Be sure to record your score on the Progress Summary Chart.

Review of Weekly Adherence Assessment

As you have been doing each week, use the Weekly Adherence Assessment Form to record any medical changes you have experienced since the last session, including changes in your symptoms, emergence of new ones, and any new test results. Rate your adherence and record it on the Progress Summary Chart.

Center for Epidemiologic Studies Depression Scale (CES-D)

Below is a list of the ways you might have felt or behaved. Please tell me how often you have felt this way during the past week.

	During the Past Week			
	Rarely or none of the time (less than 1 day)	Some or a little of the time (1–2 Days)	Occasionally or a moderate amount of time (3–4 days)	Most or all of the time (5–7 days)
1. I was bothered by things that usually don't bother me.	☐	☐	☐	☐
2. I did not feel like eating; my appetite was poor.	☐	☐	☐	☐
3. I felt that I could not shake off the blues even with help from my family or friends.	☐	☐	☐	☐
4. I felt I was just as good as other people.	☐	☐	☐	☐
5. I had trouble keeping my mind on what I was doing.	☐	☐	☐	☐
6. I felt depressed.	☐	☐	☐	☐
7. I felt that everything I did was an effort.	☐	☐	☐	☐
8. I felt hopeful about the future.	☐	☐	☐	☐
9. I thought my life had been a failure.	☐	☐	☐	☐
10. I felt fearful.	☐	☐	☐	☐
11. My sleep was restless.	☐	☐	☐	☐
12. I was happy.	☐	☐	☐	☐
13. I talked less than usual.	☐	☐	☐	☐
14. I felt lonely.	☐	☐	☐	☐
15. People were unfriendly.	☐	☐	☐	☐
16. I enjoyed life.	☐	☐	☐	☐
17. I had crying spells.	☐	☐	☐	☐
18. I felt sad.	☐	☐	☐	☐
19. I felt that people dislike me.	☐	☐	☐	☐
20. I could not get "going."	☐	☐	☐	☐

SCORING: zero for answers in the first column, 1 for answers in the second column, 2 for answers in the third colomn, 3 for answers in the fourth column. The scoring of positive items is reversed. Possible range of scores is zero to 60, with the higher scores indicating the presence of more symptomatology.

Weekly Adherence Assessment Form

You will complete this form at the start of every session. You will work with your therapist to determine your adherence goals during the Life-Steps intervention (module 2) of this treatment program.

Thinking about the **PAST WEEK**, on average how would you rate your ability to adhere to your goal of

_____?

(Check one)

Very poor	Poor	Fair	Good	Very good	Excellent
☐	☐	☐	☐	☐	☐

Thinking about the **PAST WEEK**, on average how would you rate your ability to adhere to your goal of

_____?

(Check one)

Very poor	Poor	Fair	Good	Very good	Excellent
☐	☐	☐	☐	☐	☐

Thinking about the **PAST WEEK**, on average how would you rate your ability to adhere to your goal of

_____?

(Check one)

Very poor	Poor	Fair	Good	Very good	Excellent
☐	☐	☐	☐	☐	☐

Thinking about the **PAST WEEK**, on average how would you rate your ability to adhere to your goal of

_____?

(Check one)

Very poor	Poor	Fair	Good	Very good	Excellent
☐	☐	☐	☐	☐	☐

Review of Previous Modules

Each week you should examine your progress in implementing skills from each of the previous modules. It is important to acknowledge the successes you have achieved and to problem-solve around any difficulties.

Review: CBT Model of Depression

Review your model of depression, paying close attention to how all of the components interact and contribute to your depression and problems with adhering to your medical routine and taking care of yourself. Remember, the goal of this treatment program is to break the connections between the components and help you overcome your depression.

Review: Life-Steps

Review the importance of self-care behaviors and medical adherence, as well as the AIM problem-solving technique. With the help of your therapist, make additional plans or backup plans for any new strategy that did not work for you over the previous week.

Review: Activity Scheduling

Review your completed Activity Log from the previous week with your therapist and make note of times when your mood was elevated and times when your mood was depressed. What sorts of activities made you feel good and more positive? Try to engage in these activities more often.

Review: Adaptive Thinking: Parts I and II

Review your Thought Records from the previous week and discuss with your therapist any difficulties you may be having with identifying, labeling, and challenging your automatic negative thoughts. If necessary, complete a Thought Record in session to review cognitive restructuring skills.

Review: Problem-Solving Strategies

Consider your use of the problem-solving strategy and the method for breaking down large tasks into small steps.

Breathing Retraining

The object of breathing retraining is to teach you to use calm, slow breathing in order to achieve a relaxed state. Overbreathing and chest breathing, which many people tend to do when feeling anxious, can actually make anxiety symptoms worse. Instead, it is more effective to breathe from your diaphragm. Chest breathing involves filling your lungs with air, forcing the chest upward and outward to expand, so that you are taking relatively shallow breaths. Diaphragmatic breathing, on the other hand, keeps your chest relaxed and lets the diaphragm, the smooth muscle at the bottom of the lungs, do all the work. When you inhale, the diaphragm moves down, creating a vacuum and pulling air in. This technique results in deeper breaths, which is a healthier and fuller way to take in oxygen.

Diaphragmatic Breathing Technique

In today's session, you will practice diaphragmatic breathing. Place one hand on your stomach and the other on your chest. Inhale slowly and watch which of your hands moves. If the hand on your chest moves, you are chest breathing. Diaphragmatic breathing is occurring when the hand on your stomach moves.

Get into a comfortable position. Now, slowly inhale through your nose. As you inhale, count slowly to three and feel your stomach expand with your hand. Hold the breath for one second and then slowly exhale while also counting to three. When you inhale, think of the word *inhale*. When you exhale, think of the word *relax*.

Repeat this exercise a number of times until you are able to do it correctly and effectively. Like any skill, it takes practice to master.

Some people find that they are able to do this, but only when they specifically think about it—and then go back to chest breathing when they are not specifically thinking about breathing down to their stomach. One way to work on this is to find times each day when you can practice five breaths at a time. You can go back to using the adhesive stickers from the Life-Steps module that reminded you to take your medicines and/or to think differently about medicines. When you see the stickers, make sure you are going back to stomach breathing. Do this by inhaling five times in the way just described, then go back to whatever you were doing.

Progressive Muscle Relaxation

Just like diaphragmatic breathing, muscle relaxation is a skill that can be learned as long as it is practiced regularly. It helps with stress and tension and certain side effects caused by medication, as well as pain.

Today you will do a procedure called progressive muscle relaxation, or PMR. It involves tensing, then relaxing, various muscle groups, one at a time. It takes about 25 minutes, and by the time you are done, your whole body is relaxed.

Once you are relaxed, the trick is to make a mental note of what the relaxation feels like. You can then apply this to situations of stress, in conjunction with slow breathing, when doing the whole procedure is not possible. Your therapist may make a tape of the progressive muscle relaxation procedure so that you can take it home and practice. You can also find relaxation tapes over the Internet or at local stores. After doing it with your therapist once, you can also use the outline provided to make your own recording.

Sit comfortably in the chair and relax as much as possible. Breathe calmly and regularly with your stomach. Pay attention to your therapist's voice as he or she guides you through the relaxation. You will be asked to tense and then relax your muscles systematically. When your therapist prompts you, begin tensing the muscles and holding the tension for about 5 to 10 seconds. You should tense the muscles hard enough to be aware of how they feel when they are tense. However, do not strain or hurt any muscle. The goal is to create enough tension that you will experience a clear difference between tensing and relaxation. The sequence of muscles to be tensed during PMR is outlined as follows:

- Right hand and forearm
- Left hand and forearm
- Right upper arm (bicep)
- Left upper arm (bicep)
- Neck and shoulders
- Forehead and eyes
- Lower face and jaw
- Chest and upper back
- Abdomen and lower back
- Hips, buttocks, and upper legs (right and left)
- Lower legs and feet

After you go through the entire procedure of systematically tensing and releasing/relaxing each muscle group, your therapist will help you to relax even further by instructing you to breathe calmly and regularly for a full minute. When you are fully relaxed, make a mental note of how it feels. The idea is for you to practice this technique often enough so that eventually you will be able to simply take a slow, deep breath and recover that relaxed feeling.

Muscle relaxation is a learned skill. Practice is necessary so you can master the technique and apply it in real-life situations.

Homework

✎ Continue using and reviewing skills from previous modules and sessions.

✎ Practice diaphragmatic breathing twice per day (once in the morning and once in the evening).

Breathing Retraining and Progressive Muscle Relaxation Practice Log

Relaxation Training

For each day, record whether you practiced it.
How relaxed (1–10) were you before listening to the tape?
How relaxed (1–10) were you after listening to the tape?

	Monday	Tuesday	Wednesday	Thursday	Friday	Saturday	Sunday
Morning							
Afternoon							
Evening							

Slow Breathing

For each day, place a check if you practiced slow breathing during the indicated time.

	Monday	Tuesday	Wednesday	Thursday	Friday	Saturday	Sunday
Morning							
Afternoon							
Evening							

✎ Practice progressive muscle relaxation as much as possible. Once per day is ideal, but if you can't, at least try for three to four times per week.

✎ Record your breathing exercise and relaxation training on the Breathing Retraining and Progressive Muscle Relaxation Practice Log provided.

Chapter 9 | *Review, Maintenance, and Relapse Prevention*

Goals

- To measure your progress and recognize the benefits you have achieved during your participation in this program.

- To review all the skills and strategies you have learned over the course of treatment.

- To prepare for the end of treatment by transitioning to becoming your own therapist.

Thinking About the End of Treatment

Congratulations! You have successfully completed this program and are now ready to go out on your own. However, the end of this workbook and the end of your sessions with your therapist do not equal the end of your program of treatment.

The long-term goal of this treatment is for you to learn how to implement the skills you've learned on your own. You now need to regularly practice the strategies and skills that you rehearsed as part of this program so that they become automatic. In other words, the end of regular sessions signifies the starting point of your own program of treatment and the transition to becoming your own therapist.

To begin this transition, it is important for you to recognize the nature of any benefits you have achieved. Please take some time to review your Progress Summary Chart with your therapist, as well as your completed monitoring forms (CES-D and Weekly Adherence Assessment Form). These forms will show you how much you have achieved since the start of the program. Take note of any sudden gains in treatment in the course of a given week, such as dramatic or significant reductions in your depression score or increased adherence to your medical regimen.

Table 9.1. Treatment Strategies and Usefulness Chart

Instructions: Please rate the usefulness of each strategy to you, from 0 to 100 (0 = Didn't help at all; 100 = Was extremely important for me). Also, take some time to provide notes to yourself about why you think each strategy worked or didn't work to help you, and figure out which strategies might be most helpful for you to practice over the next month.

Treatment Strategies	Usefulness Ratings	Notes About Your Application/Usefulness of Strategies
Psychoeducation Understanding the relationship between thoughts, behaviors, and physical symptoms and depression and adherence Motivational exercise: weighing pros and cons of changing vs. not changing		
Adherence Training (Life-Steps) Understanding the importance of treatment adherence Plan for transportation to medical appointments Plan for obtaining medications or other self-care items Plan for optimizing communication with medical and mental health care providers Plan for coping with side effects of medications and medical regimen Formulate a daily schedule for medications and other self-care behaviors Plan for storing medications Develop cues for taking medications or implementing other self-care procedures Prepare for adaptively coping with slips in adherence and preventing relapse		
Activity Scheduling Understand the relationship between activities and mood Incorporate activities that involve pleasure or mastery into daily schedule		

Treatment Strategies	Usefulness Ratings	Notes About Your Application/Usefulness of Strategies
Cognitive Restructuring (Adaptive Thinking) Identify automatic thoughts Identify cognitive distortions Rethink situations that make you feel bad and develop rational response to automatic thought Test automatic thoughts in real-life situations (like during a new activity) Use downward spiral technique and identify core beliefs		
Problem Solving Articulate the problem Articulate possible solutions Select the best possible solution Set a plan of action to implement the solution Break tasks into manageable steps		
Relaxation Training Diaphragmatic breathing Progressive muscle relaxation		

Usefulness of Treatment Strategies

Use the Treatment Strategies and Usefulness Chart provided to rate the usefulness of each strategy you learned throughout the course of this program on a scale of 1 to 10, where 1 = not helpful at all and 10 = most helpful. If you find that there are strategies that have not worked for you, you do not need to continue using them. However, work with your therapist to problem-solve the difficulties you had with the particular strategy or strategies and see if you can't find a way to make it more effective. If necessary, your therapist may help you to revise your goals and plans or identify entirely new strategies for you to try.

Successfully completing treatment does not mean that you will not have future difficulties with symptoms. For most conditions, symptoms and the changes you have made can wax and wane over time. The key to maintaining treatment gains over the long run is to be ready for periods of increased difficulties. These periods are not signs that the treatment has failed. Instead, these periods are signals that you need to apply the skills you learned and practice them often.

Refer back to the graph in chapter 3 (figure 3.2). Recall how it shows the difference between how most clients expect change to happen steadily and consistently in contrast to how progress usually happens, with its ebbs and flows over the sessions. At times in treatment, you may experience a worsening of symptoms or a lapse in your ability to employ behavioral skills. Remember, this is completely normal. Instead of reacting to these as failures, turn them into opportunities to gather information about what contributed to the negative change and allow for new learning.

You may use the One-Month Review Sheet provided here to refresh skills as needed. The purpose of the worksheet is to remind you of the importance of practicing skills and to help you think through which strategies might be important to practice.

Completing the review sheet may help you to prepare to recover from missing doses (or lapsing from an exercise routine, or breaking your diet regimen), which, in the long run, is likely to occur. If a lapse occurs, the best choice is to return to your adherence program as soon as possible instead of acting on hopeless thoughts and giving up. If you can identify what led to the lapse, you can prevent it from happening again in the future. Remember, lapses are normal.

Be sure to make a plan with your therapist about whether you will complete the review sheet on your own or whether you will touch base with your therapist in one month.

One-Month Review Sheet   **Date of Review:** _____

1. What skills have you been practicing well?

2. Where do you still have troubles?

3. Can you place the troubles in one of the specific domains used in this treatment?

4. Have you reviewed the chapters most relevant to your difficulties? (Which chapters are these?)

5. Have you reviewed table 9.1, where you recorded which skills were most helpful to you in the first phase of this treatment? Do you need to reapply these skills or strategies?

Troubleshooting Your Difficulties Worksheet

Symptoms	Skills to Consider
I haven't been taking my medications lately because they make me feel sick.	Review Life-Steps Skills • Life-Step 2: Communicating with treatment team • Life-Step 3: Coping with side effects
I've been spending more time alone and haven't felt like doing much lately.	Monitor activities and mood on a daily basis using Activity Log Incorporate activities that involve pleasure or mastery into daily schedule
I don't feel like going out to dinner with friends and family because I need to watch my diet and don't want to have to explain my illness to them.	Identify automatic thoughts Identify cognitive distortions Record automatic thoughts and match to distortions using Thought Record Challenge automatic thoughts and come up with a rational response
I need to lose weight but I just don't know where to start.	Practice problem-solving strategies (articulate the problem, generate possible solutions, choose the best alternative) Break tasks down into manageable steps
I get so anxious and stressed out sometimes at work and I have trouble calming down.	Diaphragmatic breathing Progressive muscle relaxation

Figure 9.1

Example of Completed Troubleshooting Your Difficulties Worksheet

Troubleshooting Your Difficulties

It may also be helpful to match some of the symptoms you may be experiencing with some of the specific strategies used in treatment. Examine figure 9.1 and see if it helps you identify some of the strategies that may be helpful to practice.

Finally, you may want to use the Problem-Solving Sheet in chapter 7 to more carefully consider any difficulties with symptoms you are currently experiencing. If these strategies do not help, consider getting additional input from family or friends or a booster session from your therapist.

Troubleshooting Your Difficulties Worksheet

Symptoms	Skills to Consider

A Final Reminder

We know completing this treatment program was a lot of hard work. However, we truly believe these skills can make a profound difference and help improve your depression and adherence. Remember the key to success is to Practice! Practice! Practice! It is essential that you continue to use all the skills you have learned in this program, even after it is over. This is the only way to make them automatic.

We wish you the best in applying your program of treatment in your life!

About the Authors

Dr. Steven Safren is an Associate Professor in Psychology at Harvard Medical School and the Director of Behavioral Medicine in the Department of Psychiatry at Massachusetts General Hospital (MGH). He also directs the cognitive-behavioral track and behavioral medicine training tracks of the MGH clinical psychology internship and is a research scientist at Fenway Community Health. Dr. Safren received his PhD in clinical psychology from the University at Albany, State University of New York, in 1998 and did his internship and postdoctoral fellowship at Massachusetts General Hospital/Harvard Medical School. Dr. Safren has over 75 professional publications. He has received several grants from the National Institutes of Health (NIH) to develop and evaluate cognitive-behavioral interventions, including two studies of cognitive-behavioral therapy for adherence and depression (CBT-AD) in patients with HIV and depression and one in patients with diabetes and depression. Additional NIH funding includes studies of CBT for adults with ADHD. Dr. Safren has served as a regular reviewer for the National Institutes of Health's study section, which reviews grants related to behavioral aspects of HIV/AIDS.

Dr. Jeffrey S. Gonzalez is a Clinical Assistant in Psychology at Massachusetts General Hospital and an Instructor in Psychology at Harvard Medical School. Dr. Gonzalez received his PhD in clinical psychology, with a specialization in health psychology, from the University of Miami. He completed his internship and postdoctoral fellowship at Massachusetts General Hospital/Harvard Medical School. In 2006 he was awarded the Early Career Award by the International Society of Behavioral Medicine. Dr. Gonzalez has 20 professional publications on behavioral medicine approaches to the study of HIV, diabetes, and cancer. He is currently co-principal investigator and project director on an NIH-funded grant to evaluate the efficacy of CBT-AD in patients with diabetes and depression. He is also a protocol therapist on both this study and a trial of CBT-AD in patients with depression and HIV. Dr. Gonzalez is a licensed psychologist specializing in behavioral medicine interventions for clients with chronic medical conditions and cognitive-behavioral therapy approaches to the treatment of mood and anxiety disorders.

Dr. Nafisseh Soroudi is a Clinical Fellow in Psychology at Massachusetts General Hospital (MGH). Dr. Soroudi received her PhD in clinical health psychology from Yeshiva University, Ferkauf Graduate School of Psychology. She completed her internship at Montefiore Medical Center and her postdoctoral fellowship at Massachusetts General Hospital/Harvard Medical School. Dr. Soroudi has six professional publications on behavioral medicine approaches to the study of HIV, obesity, and diabetes. She is currently the project director and a protocol therapist of an NIDA-funded grant to evaluate the efficacy of CBT-AD in patients with HIV and on methadone therapy. Dr. Soroudi is a clinical psychologist specializing in behavioral medicine interventions for clients and couples with chronic medical conditions and cognitive-behavioral therapy approaches to the treatment of mood and anxiety disorders.

Printed in the USA
CPSIA information can be obtained
at www.ICGtesting.com
LVHW081337191023
761407LV00004B/7

9 780195 315158